To my friend
Homer McKee,
With all Good Wishes
and Best Regards –
Dwight H. Green –

The
MIDWESTERNER

SOME BOOKS BY THE SAME AUTHORS

Robert J. Casey

THE CANNONEERS HAVE HAIRY EARS
EASTER ISLAND
FOUR FACES OF SIVA
SECRET OF 37 HARDY STREET
BAGHDAD AND POINTS EAST
I CAN'T FORGET
SUCH INTERESTING PEOPLE
TORPEDO JUNCTION
BATTLE BELOW
THIS IS WHERE I CAME IN
MORE INTERESTING PEOPLE

W. A. S. Douglas

LONG JOHN MURRAY
RACKETEERS OF EUROPE
LASSARA OF THE O'CAHANS
DARK ROSALEEN

Benjamin Z. Kanne/47—

The MIDWESTERNER

THE STORY OF
DWIGHT H. GREEN

BY

ROBERT J. CASEY

AND

W. A. S. DOUGLAS

WILCOX & FOLLETT CO.

CHICAGO   NEW YORK   TORONTO

PRINTED IN THE UNITED STATES OF AMERICA

BOOK DESIGN BY STANFORD W. WILLIAMSON

Contents

We, the jury find the defendant, Alphonse Capone, guilty. . . ."

"Let the defendant step to the bar of the court!"

Scarface Al lifts his huge body from his chair and wipes the perspiration from his face. He walks a few paces to the rostrum, locks his hands behind his back, and stares into the eyes of Federal Judge Wilkerson. The judge returns his gaze for a moment, then turns his attention to the documents in front of him and begins to recount the penalties provided by the law under which the gangster has been convicted.

Capone shuffles his feet, coughs softly once, and stands in a half-slouch. Occasionally his fingers twitch. His lips are thrust outward in a characteristic pout. . . . .

"It is the judgment of this court that on count one the defendant serve five years in the custody of the attorney general or his authorized agent, pay a fine of $10,000 and the costs of the prosecution. . . . ."

Capone winces. . . . .

". . . . . that on count five the defendant serve five years in the custody of the attorney general or his authorized agent, pay a fine of $10,000 and the costs of the prosecution. . . . .

Al Capone's ending — Dwight Green's beginning.

". . . . . that on count nine . . . ." and so, for a total of eleven years in the penitentiary, $50,000 in fines and another $50,000 [costs]. . . . .

"The marshall will take the defendant into custody....."
Public enemy No. 1 leaves the courtroom in handcuffs
on his way to Atlanta — later to Alcatraz. As he is hustled
through one door, a stockily built young man, the hair at
his temples already touched with grey, slowly picks up
his papers, departs through another door.

1

FIREMAN, SAVE THAT CHILD

TIME SEEMS TO HAVE BEGUN FOR LIGONIER, INDIANA, on the day when Pete Green, aged four, rang a general alarm on the fire bell at the top of the fire tower with his little red hatchet.

Other things had happened to Ligonier before that time. Other things have happened to Pete Green since. But local history, with a nice sense of the dramatic and important, has made no particular note of them.

You go into this mellow old town to learn something of the influences that shaped the character and career of a lad who a few years after leaving home had become one of the most talked of lawyers in the United States, had broken the back of the Capone syndicate, and had been elected Governor of Illinois to the surprise of everybody including his party leaders. Everybody in Ligonier knows him and all about him just as everybody in Ligonier has known everybody else in Ligonier for a hundred years.

The old ladies of the community can give you chapter and verse on most of his life from the day he was born till the day he went away to college. They can tell you what kind of clothes his mother put on him when he was three, what sort of diet he was given as a baby, how he performed in the annual exhibit of the high-school dramatic society. A few aging teachers can — and will — recite from memory what sort of marks he made in arithmetic and spelling and geometry and Latin and history. The members of the "Hot Stove League" of Will Sacks' grocery store in Cavin Street are walking scrapbooks of information about his career during the last ten or fifteen years in the big city. If you want to go into details, most of them know what his Chicago street address was in 1933, what offices he worked in when he was studying law, what size collar he wore when he was thirty-five years old, how he stood in the Wabash College debating society, what his weekly wages amounted to for hauling lumber in Indianapolis the summer before World War I, and what he did in the air corps. They recall his record in semiprofessional baseball and as an occasional member of the barbershop quartet — not always in terms of praise: "He was a sucker for a low incurve." "He sang loud and he stayed on the key; but he was no Caruso." But when you get any or all of these people together and ask them a general question about the life and times of Dwight Herbert Green (the onetime "Pete") you come back to the fire bell. It seems to have sounded its tocsin in the spring of 1901, but so far as Ligonier is concerned it is still ringing.

Ligonier, like most American towns of its size and time, had a volunteer fire department consisting of a couple of hose carts, a hand pump, and a lot of earnest but amateur firemen. It had no telegraph alarm system, no central telephone switchboard over which the faithful firefighters could be mobilized quickly in their waterproof hats. As a practical substitute it had a "fire tower," a structure like a windmill, on top of which hung a length of railroad iron. In an emergency it was customary for some agile citizen to shin up a sixty-foot ladder and beat the railroad iron with a maul or other suitable implement.

This, of course, brought the news of the fire not only to the fire department but to the entire citizenry. And that was considered fair enough because everybody in town was interested in fires; public amusements weren't any too frequent.

Our Mr. Pete Green got the idea of the thing at an early age. At three the clanging of the gong would bring him tearing into the house, where he would plead, or bawl, until somebody took him out to enjoy the spectacle of the strangely costumed fire department helping somebody's barn to burn down. He didn't seem to have been exactly certain whether or not the beating of the alarm was the actual cause of the fire. But the connection between the din and the flames was obvious.

His friends recall that during most of his third year and all of his fourth his mother had no trouble keeping track of him. He might wander away from home, as little boys of his age are said to do, but his parents always knew where to find him. He would be found standing at the foot of the "fire tower" studying the problem of cause and effect, which he lacked words to explain to his sometimes exasperated elders.

The MIDWESTERNER

The logbook of the Ligonier fire department shows that things were very quiet during the first four or five months of 1901. "Pete" made his daily pilgrimage to the "fire tower," for then as now he appears to have been persistent. Consistent disappointment doesn't seem to have soured him any or to have altered his belief that the inevitable is sure to happen if you wait long enough. But as he got older—which is to say four years of age—he acquired a lot of collateral ideas. One of these, which seems to be proof against argument, was that if you want a thing done you'll get faster results if you start it off yourself.

Pete's birthday was January 9th, and on that important day one of his presents was a small dull hatchet. It would be nice here to say something of the cherry orchards in the vicinity of his home. But unfortunately there weren't any cherry trees, he was too young to have been influenced by any of the current legends concerning cherry trees, and furthermore that sort of a hatchet wouldn't have got him far in woodcraft anyway. He chopped ineffectually at one thing or another around his own backyard for what remained of the winter and then got a new idea.

One bright afternoon in June the Yoders and Sackses and Bauers and Strauses and Schildhauers and other members of the fire department were aroused from sundry jobs and conversations by the insistent and erratic ringing of the alarm. As was customary in such emergencies, they listened carefully for the code of quick and slow strokes that would tell them what part of town was furnishing the fire. But there wasn't any code—only a protracted loud and frantic beating that could indicate only one thing. The whole town must be going up in flames at once.

[4]

There are no available statistics concerning how long it ought to take a volunteer fireman to get into his hat. But the old-timers who remember that day in vivid detail are convinced that they saw the establishment of an unbreakable world's record for the event. Not only the firemen but every able-bodied adult was dashing for the firehouse in a matter of split seconds. The lame and the halt and the aged and the very young children came later.

Perhaps at the beginning of it all there was a moment of panic. There might well have been as the alarm continued to bang out its dire background music like the drums in Emperor Jones. There were still people in Ligonier who had seen the great Chicago fire. And enough local buildings had made sizeable ash piles to keep the populace generally aware of what such catastrophes meant.

On the other hand even a four-eleven fire alarm ceases to be alarming when nothing is burning. All the business section of the town, and for a place of the size there was quite a lot of it, was cool and intact. There wasn't a wisp of smoke in the sky nor a hint of burning wood in the still air. The hundreds of folks who in two or three minutes after the first clang were sniffing diligently with upturned noses detected nothing more terrifying than a not unusual scent of hay.

Somewhat dazedly the lay citizenry followed the glistening hats of the fire department in a more or less leisurely trot up the hill.

At the fire tower they found the answer which, considering signs that virtually anybody might have interpreted during the preceding five or six months, wasn't so surprising after all. On top of the tower, teetering on the unrailed platform like a sailor in a high wind, stood Pete Green getting some real use out of his little red hatchet.

What happened next is what the old-timers remember rather than the threat of a major fire. Pete Green was up there and some hundreds of people began to wonder immediately how Pete Green was going to get down. Anyone climbing up after him might frighten him. Anyone calling to him might cause him to make a misstep on his precarious roost. The entire crowd stood suddenly motionless and silent, afraid to draw a breath.

About this time along came Mrs. Harry Green, looking for her son and well aware, as she had been from the first moment after the sounding of the gong, where she was going to find him. With no outward show of concern she worked her way quietly through the mass of spectators till she came to the foot of the ladder. Then in the same voice she might have used to summon him to dinner she called:

"It's all right now, Dwight. The fire's out and you can come down."

Pete stuck his little red hatchet into his belt and clambered down to receive what acclaim the multitude was waiting to give him. What happened to him after his mother had taken him gently by the hand and led him home is something nobody seems to remember. It is significant that he ceased his visits to the tower and that Ligonier from that day to this has never again known the threat of disaster, but it is also significant that he never again had to empty all the houses in town to make the citizenry aware of his existence. He was henceforth one of the town celebrities.

"Pete Green," reminisced Will Sack forty-seven years later, "Yes, of course, he's governor of Illinois. . . . . Certainly everybody knows about how he finished Al Capone and prosecuted Sam Insull. But he didn't have to get into the metropolitan newspapers to keep his memory alive down here. Everybody in this county knows him. Did anybody ever tell you about the time he rang the fire alarm with his little red hatchet? . . . ."

2

LIGONIER BEGINNING

LIGONIER HAD BEEN RECOGNIZED AS A PLACE OF considerable historical background long before little Pete Green began his bell ringing. You don't find many commemorative placques scattered about, nor iron horsemen brandishing sabers in the park. It was the scene of no great battles, and a lot of recent G.I.'s discount the idea that anything ever happened in it worth mentioning. But for all that it is a place of traditions such as you are likely to find nowhere else in Indiana. For the pioneers who settled this area came with a definite purpose and brought with them their own traditions. The history of their principles and ambitions and culture did not suffer any through transplantation.

John Cavin, who does not figure much in any of the local folklore, founded Ligonier some time in the eighteen forties. After the fashion of most of the town planners of his time he named it for the place from which he had come

— Ligonier in Pennsylvania. Today, few people know that Ligonier, Pennsylvania, was christened for a street in Belfast, Northern Ireland.

But this quiet, unhurried, conservative town actually came into being as the result of a bitter and bloody revolution in Germany. That this event occurred thousands of miles away didn't diminish its effect on the building of a part of northern Indiana, nor alter its importance to the financial and political future of the United States.

In 1848 a number of hitherto uncomplaining and placid citizens of the Grand Duchy of Baden became as tired of their government as generations of Germans have since had reason to be. They declared a republic, exiled the Grand Duke and began a movement which, had it succeeded, might well have prevented a couple of ghastly wars and made the modern world a better place to live in. But it didn't succeed. The monarchy, generously assisted by the artillery of Frederick of Prussia, came back to power and the whole incident was squeezed into a couple of paragraphs in history.

However, whether or not it did anything to change the destiny of Germany, it began to have an immediate influence on population trends in the United States. Not only in Baden, but in all the other states that Bismarck was presently to dovetail into an empire, the political reformers realized that there was no hope for the establishment of a democracy in Germany. Following the exhortations of such men as Carl Schurz, they sold their possessions or merely abandoned them and came to America in thousands to become the country's most militant supporters of democratic progress. And part of this vast exodus of liberals from a country that has not yet recovered from their loss were the German families who presently found themselves in the raw, new country around the town John Cavin of Ligonier, Pennsylvania built.

Along with Christian Germans came Jewish Germans trickling into northern Indiana. Among the first of these latter settlers was a family named Straus, in which there were two notable brothers, Isaac and Simon, and their father Jacob. Jacob was a pack trader, plodding endlessly through the neighboring country, which was then little more than a sparsely populated wilderness. The Strauses prospered. Their friends and relatives came to join them, lured not so much by the news of their success in business as by the cumulative evidence that this was a community where it was safe to go to a synagogue, and murder was something more than a week-end exercise for Prussian cavalry.

The German Jewish immigration had interesting results. At one period, around the time of the Civil War, Ligonier and its environs contained a larger proportion of Jewish settlers than was to be found in any other community in the United States. There was a flourishing synagogue in the town, and a couple of hundred Jewish children in the local school. Jewish merchants did more than half the business in Cavin Street, and the records of that period show not a single case of religious, social, or racial strife.

The Green family, in so far as the United States is concerned, had its beginning in Henry Green, who was born in Germany, in 1833, and came to the United States in 1853. He first joined an uncle who a few years previously had settled on a farm near Massillon, Ohio.

The uncle liked Henry and thought he might make a good farm hand. Henry thought so, too, and the whole saga of the Green family might have been altered irrevocably if he had ever learned the uses of an old-fashioned implement known to the trade as a horse weight.

He had been in Massillon nearly two years when one day he was given an assignment to take his three young girl cousins riding in a spring wagon. Somewhere along the route he got out of the wagon and forgot to drop the weight. More than that he forgot to wrap the reins around the whip socket. The bored horse, quick to notice this opportunity, lit out for home, spilling little girls all over the landscape.

The girls weren't damaged beyond a few negligible bruises. But Henry, who led the tearful procession home, had worse luck. His uncle expressed such a poor opinion of his talents and prospects that he packed his suitcase and went to Cincinnati, where he got a job trimming hams for a packing plant.

When the Civil War began he enlisted and was assigned to the quartermaster corps depot of the Union army at St. Louis. He was promoted gradually to the rating of commissary sergeant. While still in uniform he married Miss Magdalene Kaul, also of German birth, and brought her to Ligonier, where he remained continuously until his death in 1900.

His well-worn family Bible, printed in German, records the birth of three sons: Frederick Henry, John Henry, and Harry. Harry was to be the father of Dwight Green.

Henry prospered. With what money he had saved during the war and a little inheritance that he received from

Germany, he bought 80 acres of land outside the town to raise cattle for the city markets. He fitted easily into the life of Ligonier, which, after all, wasn't much different from that of the town he'd come from in Germany. Most of his neighbors were compatriots, and the old customs and traditions survived for a long time.

With what remained of his capital he opened a meat market that stayed in business nearly fifty years, until the last of his family died or moved away.

There are still marks of the original German influence on the town as it exists today — wide streets, broad, tree-shaded lawns, and a general air of neatness. There is quiet beauty in the residence districts — comfortable, well-kept houses, trim gardens, and more than a passing suggestion of fresh paint and laundry soap.

The so-called wilderness was quickly vanishing when Henry Green arrived to open his butcher shop. The rush of population toward the West was following the railroad. The patches of forest were being swept into sawmills to spread a tide of plank-and-shingle villages along the lonesome routes of the early peddlers. In the sense that pioneering meant a life of constant discomfort, infrequent food, isolation from the civilized world, lack of medical care and human contacts, and a constant fear of violence from disgruntled redskins, the day of the pioneer was already done.

There was business in all of these communities now that goods could be hauled cheaply for hundreds of miles, big business as such things would have been rated in villages of similar size in Europe. Beyond the horizon, Chicago was rising out of a swamp to be one of the great cities of the world. There was a constant market there for almost anything that could be shipped into it — corn, cattle, fruit, wool, horses, lumber. And there, in warehouses that seemed likely to go on expanding forever, the early settlers of Indiana could make deals in money if they had it, in produce if they had not, for everything that made life comfortable, not to say luxurious, in the metropolis of the lakes.

Ligonier in the fifties probably was just another oil town without the oil. Unlike the hamlets that voyagers from the Cumberlands had built in southern Indiana with an eye to mutual protection and interchange of labor and rudimentary barter, it was no cluster of rude log cabins with mud floors and plaited leather bed springs and rush-lights and glassless windows. It was rather a seething assemblage of unpainted plank shacks furnished with the latest gewgaws from Field & Leiter's, awninged stores with false fronts and fabulous stocks of eye-catching gimcracks, rutted streets that were dusty or fetlock-deep in mud — depending on the weather — a fair collection of wooden churches, a barnlike opera house, and an overcrowded bank. Only the inherent traits of the populace kept it from being the exact counterpart of any town that set down its expectant roots in that vanished West now so vividly portrayed in the horse-and-buggy exhibits.

Nowdays there is no lavish display of wealth in Ligonier. You have to look for it under simple surfaces. The bank buildings are modest. One of the town's most important business houses gets along quite well without so much as a sign on the window to identify it. At least two million-aires live here in virtual seclusion in houses devoid of grilled balconies and cupolas or other affectations which in other parts of the state seem to have been prescribed by law for the punishment of the very rich.

But in the beginning the wealth was right out where everybody could see it — herds of cattle plodding down Cavin Street in choking clouds of dust, bales of wool on the platforms of the railroad station, long wagon trains of farm produce constantly riding over the brow of the hill. There is a legend that everybody was well off in those days, and it isn't hard to believe. Chicago was a magic box into which you dumped things — anything — and found them presently turned to gold.

Such was the shack bonanza into which Henry Green brought his German-born wife, and he never had any reason to regret the impulse that led him there.

3

MUSIC CENTER

IT IS LIKELY THE LINGUA FRANCA OF THE DISTRICT
when Henry Green became part of it was mostly
German. The Germans seldom had to speak with
anyone save other Germans or the Jews, to whom a foreign
language has never presented any great difficulty. Or it
may have been that the populace contrived some sort of
workable esperanto out of German and Hebrew and
Yiddish.

It is significant of the patriotism and practicality of the
community, however, that whatever language was used
in the days of its first development, the second generation
spoke English and nothing else. No attempt was made,
even for sentimental reasons to preserve the tongue of
the homeland collaterally. There were German courses in
the schools, just as there were courses in Latin and Greek
for those who wanted them, but only for academic purposes.

Ligonier began to take on the look of permanence that is its most striking characteristic some time in the seventies. Most of the wealth that had flowed in so continuously during the boom days had been conserved through careful investment in land and livestock and business. Despite the ups and downs of the national economy in one of the dizziest periods of the country's history, the local per capita wealth increased, sometimes slowly but always steadily. The banks were sound and prosperous. Perhaps nobody was very rich according to modern standards. But on the other hand nobody was poor. Social and commercial intercourse were marked by no serious rivalries — few evidences of envy.

Discounting the shortened perspective of the graybeards, all of whom in every time and every clime seem to have passed their fruitful years in a sort of flawless Arcady, it seems safe to say this was a region of considerably more than average comfort and happiness. Everybody worked hard and ceaselessly, but nobody made any complaint about that. It was the custom to work. No matter how much money one might have, it would be considered a serious error if he didn't work. Not only in Ligonier but in all other parts of the restless nation the loafer was classed with the drunkard as a parasite and a nuisance. If you worked, you prospered and you were able to provide your family with benefits you could never have dreamed of for yourself.

Once the financial status of Ligonier was established the "sham and shingles" architecture of John Cavin's boom town began to disappear. Brick and stone replaced the plank boxes in the business section. More and more money went into homes and substantial churches were erected to care for the needs of "virtually every religious sect under the sun except the Mohammedan and Shinto." A permanent theater took the place of the old wooden barn that had been the opera house. A music hall, fitted with soft carpets and plush furniture and quantities of highly polished brass cuspidors, was built, not for the profit of any greedy entrepreneur, but as a municipal contribution to the fostering of the arts. It was reputed to be the finest of its kind in the middle west. And history shows that it was worth all that it cost.

Outside of school and home entertainments and the usual run of family parties, there weren't many amusements in the Ligonier of the eighties and nineties.

Books were plentiful and intelligently read. Political subjects were vital, as they generally are in a new community, and tirelessly discussed. Newspapers came daily from Chicago and Toledo. The isolation of Ligonier, if one may call it that, was geographical, not mental. Everybody who had finished the sixth reader knew what was going on in the world and was able to talk about it. And above all this in the inventory of the community's cultural assets was an almost universal feeling for music.

There is some practical explanation for this manifestation quite aside from inherited traits that the founders of the town had brought with them from the old country. In the patternless development of the region a factory had been set up for the production of band instruments at Elkhart, twenty-odd miles to the northeast on the railroad.

It brought in professional musicians in considerable numbers to rest briefly at resorts in lake regions or to idle away the winter months in the towns.

The musicians, as is usual with their craft, weren't interested in much of anything but music. They argued music among themselves, talked of it freely with anyone who would listen. In the bars and barbershops and hotel lobbies and stores of Ligonier they tirelessly spread the propaganda of their difficult art. They found a ready and receptive audience. Most of the local males and half the females began to develop their musical talents on flutes and harps and trombones and pianos and cornets until virtually everybody in town could give a creditable performance on one instrument or another, and the music hall was built to comply with a great popular demand.

The amazing thing about this particular renaissance was that, like the aging brick blocks of Cavin Street, it had good foundations and permanence. An unbelievably large number of first-class technicians emerged from the preliminary chaos of practice. The standards of performance reached such heights that the bulk of the less gifted amateurs refrained from rushing into public performance, and the little Salzburg of Ligonier became easy to hear and worth hearing.

A town band was organized — as might have been expected. But, unlike most town bands, it turned out to be a good one. In the middle eighties it was a better box-office attraction than the best of the visiting road shows. By 1890 it had the stature, if not the official recognition, of a first-class philharmonic society.

Probably the most thoroughly artistic musicians in town at the time of the formation of the band were to be found in the Sack family. The original Sack, another German who wanted to live in a democracy, came into Ligonier on the heels of John Cavin — not as a troubadour but as a grocer. He opened a store which is still in business, still operated by a member of his family, after ninety years. He didn't need the urging of visiting professionals to become interested in music. His grandfather and father before him had been musicians, and it was not particularly remarkable that their talents should have come down to him.

It isn't remarkable at all that there is no record of Ligonier's first Sack as a working musician. But it is little short of amazing that he brought up his children in the old traditions of the family. They would have to pay twice as much attention to artistic development as might ordinarily have been demanded of them, he said, to make up for his own enforced defection. And they did. Two of them, Chris and William, were still running the family grocery store in the eighties — a job that entailed about ten hours a day of fairly hard labor. But for all the handicap of their environment the pair of them were the outstanding musicians of the entire region, which is a way of saying that one would have to look a long time before finding better. One was about as good as the other, and they took turns directing the local symphonists.

Until the nineties the audiences that the band could reach were limited. Every member was making a living at something else. He practiced when his work permitted. He was able to travel only over the week ends, and then only a few miles from home. Small neighboring towns turned out to the concerts en masse. Home-town enthusiasts stood in the street outside the music hall to catch what they could of rehearsals. But the reputation of the organization spread eastward only about as far as Kendallville and was little more than a rumor in South Bend.

This was the situation in 1893 when the directors of the World's Columbian Exposition in Chicago announced the details of an international band contest. It offered numerous attractive prizes, but that wasn't what interested Ligonier so much as the fact that it would be open to any musical groups, professional or amateur, able to qualify after a preliminary audition. Ligonier promptly sent in an entry blank.

Will Sack was ill when the time arrived for the competition, and he couldn't make the trip. But he made a short speech to the players as his brother Chris lined them up for their march to the railroad station.

"There's no use playing the popular stuff," he told them. "Maybe you do that best, maybe not. But I don't think the judges will be expecting you to play the classics as well as you do. Just be as good as you'd want to be in a Sunday evening concert in the Methodist church, and you'll get a prize."

So they went to Chicago, and they did what he'd told them to do. They played the second movement from Beethoven's Fourth Symphony. They got first prize against the competition of 3,000 other bands! The boys came home to their fine music hall with a medal that gave them official rating as the best band in the world. The population of the town that had produced this phenomenon was at that time something less than 2,000, about evenly divided, as was the membership of the band, between Gentiles and Jews.

Harry Green was one of the numerous local contingent who made the trip to Chicago for the contest. He played no musical instrument himself, at least not in public. His people were like the majority of the folks in Ligonier; they were intensely interested in what has been called the most subtle of the arts. They had had a thorough grounding in it from childhood. They were proud of the bandsmen who were as good as they would wish them to be. But their ears were too good to permit any self-deception concerning their own technical talents. So Harry went along as a sort of tour conductor and business manager. His concern in the affair was just as great as if he'd been playing a difficult part on the E-flat cornet.

The award to the band was his award, just as it was the personal award of every adult in Ligonier — which seems fair enough. The band wasn't just a collection of twenty or thirty mechanics skilled in getting sounds out of brass. It was the summation of a love of art, the epitome of a widespread culture. The band was Ligonier and Ligonier was the band. And now Ligonier had been recognized internationally as something unique among the small towns of the world.

— 4 —

THE HOD CARRIER

HARRY, JOHN, AND FRED GREEN VIRTUALLY GREW up in their father's meat market. John and Fred, the elder brothers, received only a grade-school education, but Harry was luckier. The high school was opened just as he finished eighth grade, and he went on for another four years. All of the boys worked in the market, Harry as well as the others, from the time they were able to weigh out a pound of meat, whether they were going to school or not. For the business continued to expand year after year, and Henry Green was a firm believer in family enterprise.

He was something of a patriarchal figure in other ways, too. He was the advisor if not the arbiter of his sons' affairs long after they had come to manhood. He directed their politics:

"Vote Republican. That's a very good general rule. If you find a Democrat running for office who's better quali-

fied than the Republican running against him, well, vote for
the Democrat for the time being. That's just good common
sense. But don't get into the habit of it. There are always
enough good Republicans around except for some occasional mischance." He directed them in the ways of frugality and decent living. "A man's family is his first concern.
..... No man ever makes so much money that he can afford
to throw it away. You can't waste a dollar without making
a place where you can waste two." And to some extent at
least he directed their marriages: "Get married young. A
young man with a wife has no time for nonsense. He will
prosper because he has reason to prosper." But he wasn't a
martinet. His sons loved and respected him, and none of
them had any reason to regret that they took his advice.
It proved out in later years.

In 1891 Harry married Miss Minnie Gerber, daughter of
Eli Baron Gerber, another local figure of surprising and
varied talent. Eli Gerber was a civil engineer who had come
up the hard way from an obscure and difficult boyhood in
a pioneer home near Canton, Ohio, where he was born in
1831. He had received a smattering of normal learning in
the common schools of the region, but secured most of his
education out of books, though books were expensive and
hard to get.

By 1855 he was a qualified engineer and he went west
looking for somebody who might need his talents. The
west, as he found it, wasn't much concerned with engineers.
With great tracts of land open to settlement, few villages
of more than a couple of dozen houses, and no interest in
accurate boundaries or property locations, surveyors
weren't in great demand.

But he did get one job. He stayed for a while in a town on the Missouri that had what must have seemed delusions of grandeur. The little village, like the eohippus that wanted to be a horse, decided to be a city. It was manifestly out of order that a city should be allowed to grow haphazardly. So Gerber was hired to plot a city that consisted of a nuclear hamlet, unbounded hope, and about 100,000 location stakes. He made a good job of it, before he packed up to go back east. The plan he left is in use, unchanged, today. The name of the cocksure village was Omaha, Nebraska.

Gerber realized that the farther west he went, the fewer would be the towns with big ideas. Even when he had reached the more civilized settlements of northern Indiana, he could see no immediate future in engineering. He laid up his target and transit and stopped at Ligonier to become the lone teacher in the little red schoolhouse.

He turned carpenter after that and built the first Methodist Episcopal church and other buildings in the neighborhood while waiting for a return of public interest in engineering. It came with the increase in population, and for ten years he served as county surveyor. During that period he made maps of Noble County and counties adjoining and alternated this work with a service on the board of education that gave Ligonier its first high school. Probably more than anybody else in the community he had the stature, spirit, and adaptability of the rare breed of men who made the West.

Minnie Gerber seems to have inherited many of her father's characteristics. Certainly she had plenty of his wisdom in the rearing of her children — a great deal of his gift for seeing into the future and his philosophy that nobody can have too much education. That she was in complete harmony with the life of this remarkable town where she and Harry lived in one of the most comfortable houses on Main Street is not surprising. She had been a part of it since her birth.

The Harry Greens had two children, Mary Magdalene, born in 1893, and Dwight, "Pete," born in 1897. Mary was no particular bother. She was a bright and pleasant child, with all of her brother's liveliness and gift for making friends. But she fortunately lacked his streak of inventiveness.

Dwight, or "Pete" as he is more generally known locally, although the purpose of his rechristening is somewhat obscure, had what he still believes to have been the typical upbringing of a boy in any small town in these United States. The things that made Ligonier anything but "typical" as small towns go could not be noticed by one who had no basis for comparison. Little Pete logically got the idea that all business districts were like Cavin Street, all populations were fifty per cent Jewish, all people liked music and had a lot of it, all people read hundreds of books, all grownups knew quite a lot about everything and could talk interestingly about pretty nearly everything.

Pete Green was four years old when he rang the fire bell with his little hatchet and the wise heads of Ligonier realized that he was on his way. Where he might end, they weren't yet prepared to say. But there wasn't any doubt that he was going. They got their next indication of his progress when, at the age of five, he became a hod carrier.

Almost as many folks remember this as remember the band that was "the best in the world." Novelty is what makes for public interest, and there never had been a five-year-old hod carrier before and probably never has been since.

About the time of Dwight's birth the townsfolk had grown tired of battling the mud and dust of Cavin Street. Somebody had suggested to the council that it might be a good thing to pave the street to the top of the hill at the south end of town. The subject came in for the customary mulling over and opposition, but finally the contract was let and Eli Gerber took over the work.

After the incident of the fire tower Pete hadn't been allowed to do much journeying by himself, but he didn't notice the supervision. He tagged along with his grandfather in and out of town, an arrangement that he would have preferred to any other, anyway.

The street paving interrupted what had been a fine association. Grandpa Gerber didn't seem to be going anywhere anymore. He just stood around and watched a lot of men driving teams and carrying bricks. After a couple of days all this business bored Pete almost to tears, but he found out that if he didn't want to help his grandfather watch the bricklayers, somebody would take him to his home — a block away from the project — and coop him up in the house or in the back yard. And that was no choice at all.

In time it occurred to him that there must be some fun carrying brick, so many people seemed to be doing it. He mentioned to Grandpa Gerber that he'd like to share in the excitement.

"So you want to be a hod carrier," asked his grandfather.

The Hod Carrier

"I want to carry bricks," said Pete. "I can carry bricks. Every day at my house my mamma lets me carry bricks."

"We can always use a good hand," Mr. Gerber told him. "You're hired. You can start now."

"You must get me mitts, white ones," Pete demanded. "Everybody has white mitts when they carry bricks. But I haven't any white mitts. You must get me some white mitts."

"I knew there was a catch in this business," said Grandpa Gerber.

Dwight was right about the white mitts. All the professional hod carriers wore them, canvas ones that came in two sizes, large and larger. Nowhere in town was there a pair that would fit the hands of a five-year-old hod carrier.

"This looks like a job for your mother," Mr. Gerber decided. So he took Pete home, where Mrs. Green cut out a pair of mitts and ran them up on the sewing machine.

In fifteen minutes the future Governor of Illinois was embarked on his first job, carrying bricks one at a time from a large pile to places where they could be of no possible use. His hours were flexible. He staged frequent sit-down strikes. His aptness at getting in the way of less important workmen who didn't wear tailor-made mitts amounted to sabotage. But he worked every day. When the paving reached the top of the hill and stopped, he was paid twelve cents, probably at the current scale for man-hours put in.

His mother put the pennies into a special piggy bank and he kept them until they disappeared — along with the toil-stained mitts — at a political meeting when he was running for Mayor of Chicago. It is the studied opinion of those

around him that the loot probably fell into the hands of a
needy Democrat. But one can't be sure. In those days the
Republicans were pretty needy, too.

At the age of six he had to go to school, which ended
his prospects in the brick-carrying business. Near him in
the first grade sat Herman Sack, one of the famous family
of musicians. They became friends and were inseparable
companions until Dwight left to go into the air corps in
the First World War. Both of them knew considerable about
music and liked it. They wouldn't have been children of
Ligonier if they hadn't. But by the time they'd reached
third grade, they had come to look upon the arts as a matter
of secondary interest. What concerned them most was
baseball, which Dwight had heard was a very fine thing
because somebody paid you for playing. Herman was
dubious. All the kids he knew had been playing at one thing
or another for years, and they hadn't collected a cent for it.

In this phase of young Dwight Green's thought we
come upon another of the strangely assorted elements that
combined to make up the Ligonier culture. Some local
lad had left the town to play first base with Baltimore or
some other professional league team, and from time to
time he had brought back to the old town tales of amazing
interest. The little boys of that generation absorbed this
lore and passed it on to other boys, and it continued to
circulate long after the identity of the original author had
become an uncertain memory.

Whether it was that the conversation of the small fry
tended to focus the ambitions of lads getting ready to step
into the world beyond the New York Central Railroad
station or that the soil of Noble County nourishes baseball

players as that of Kentucky does race horses, we don't know. But Ligonier has furnished more than its quota of professional players to the major leagues. There were, for instance, Bill Inks who played on the White Sox team and his brother Bert who for years pitched for Connie Mack. And behind them there was always the dim figure of the lad who played first base for Baltimore.

Once you've spent a few evenings with the hot-stove league that meets in Will Sack's 90-year-old grocery store, you can explain the effects of the local obsession if not its origins. You understand that as a schoolboy in Ligonier, Pete Green could no more have escaped an interest in baseball than he could have escaped an acquaintance with counterpoint at fugue. Music, literature, the standing of the Cubs — he heard about one or another or all of them whenever anybody started to talk. It might have made him remember that the Romans had produced great architecture and gladiators virtually without a change of stance. But it was all too familiar a business to him to occasion any analytical thought. If baseball, music, and literature were the three important and related arts in Ligonier, well, weren't they so everywhere else in the wide world?

In all biographies of public figures one notes a universal purposefulness, if not omniscience, in each biography. Somebody in chapter one says to the boy Washington, "And what are you going to be when you grow up, my little man?" And the little man knows the right answer. "I, sir," he says politely, "am going to be the Father of my country."

It would be nice, if, in looking over the background of Dwight Green, one could discover him forecasting that he was going to send Al Capone to Alcatraz and get himself elected Governor of Illinois and perform other deeds of high emprise. But unfortunately the only question-and-answer record dealing with anything connected with the matter doesn't read that way.

When he was just about ready to get out of the eighth grade at the age of fourteen his mother made the customary inquiry.

"Well," said Dwight Green, "that's something I've been thinking over pretty carefully. I think I'll be a big-league baseball player."

Young Dwight was a lad of imagination. When he was about ten, he and Herman Sack and a number of boys in their room at school arranged to give what they called "a small circus" in the Greens' barn. Most of these boys were small, but Jake Sheets, one lad who accompanied them on all their expeditions, had fairly large bones and was just beginning to expand. His presence in "the small circus" presented something of a problem.

"He'll bust things," said Herman Sack. "He's almost twice as heavy as the rest of us, and he doesn't know it."

"I like him," said Dwight.

"So do I like him," said Herman. "But that don't change the fact that he's too big for this show."

The production committee sat down and considered the matter. Of course it would have been simple to send a delegation to tell Jake to stay away from the show entirely. But that, they feared, might cause him to think he wasn't wanted. Dwight Green considered this phase of the difficulty for some time. Then as usual he got an idea.

"I'll fix it," he said. "He won't be in the show and nobody will hurt his feelings. Just leave it to me."

They left it to him. The show was next afternoon, but when Jake showed up half an hour ahead of the scheduled starting time the gang had already arrived. Every normal entrance to the barn had been closed and nailed shut. But in the big carriage door, Pete had sawed out a smaller door through which he and his cast and a number of spectators chosen for size could slip in and out with no great difficulty. But Jake couldn't make it. Pete had measured his more bulky areas with great care.

A year later the big circus came to town and brought with it one of the greatest inspirations in Dwight's hometown career. The circus wasn't much different from others he had seen with fair regularity for a number of years — the usual array of acrobats, clowns, bareback riders, and elephants. But it had one attraction the like of which had never been shown in this part of Indiana before.

From near the top of the tent in one ring a troughlike runway curved down and up again. Midway of the rising grade was a break of some five feet after which the trough resumed its course upward a few feet then sloped gently downward to sawdust level. Over this contraption as a climax to each day's performance rode a man in spangled tights astride a bicycle. He would plummet from the top at a dizzy speed, take the rise, leap the gap to the next runway, lose momentum on the next hill, and coast with leisurely grace down into the arena. Dwight Green saw this exhibition twice and each time thought it was the most thrilling thing he had ever encountered.

On the following Saturday he called the usual assemblage of kids into his yard and directed them while they hauled a number of iron coal chutes out of the basement. His mother heard him talking about something being easy, but the customary warning bell failed to tinkle in her brain and she went on with her housework.

Meanwhile Dwight thought himself lucky to find most of the material for a splendid apparatus so close at hand. Two of the chutes were given approximately the right slants with sawhorses in the backyard. A third was taken upstairs while Mrs. Green was doing something in the basement laundry. This chute was tied with clothesline to the rafters so that it slanted out the rear attic window, pointing in the general direction of those set in place below. Then Pete Green went downstairs and got his velocipede.

At that moment a belated intuition caused his mother to start up from the basement on the run. When she got to the attic she caught a glimpse of Pete starting down the chute on his tricycle. She threw herself forward and caught him by the seat of the pants just as he was headed over the sill. The velocipede went on and crashed in the yard.

It was a total wreck. But Pete wasn't disturbed about that. He'd outgrown it anyway.

5

CHOOSING A PROFESSION

S O WENT THE IDYLLIC DAYS OF WHAT DWIGHT GREEN remembers as "the average boyhood of an average boy in a small town." His uncle John Henry Green, who now lives in Milwaukee, doesn't agree that there was anything average about it. It is his vivid recollection, to be specific, that "young Pete was the damndest kid who had been seen around the place since the Indians went away." But no matter. Young Pete's luck continued to keep pace with his inventiveness, and "average" or not, he managed to survive and eventually to achieve a permanent place in Ligonier's extensive folklore.

Outwardly at least, he made some effort to conform to the community's design for living. Following the best local traditions, he studied music and although he never was admitted to the company of the elect in Concert Hall he became a better-than-average pianist. He had a good ear, a good memory, and an instinctive understanding of the mathematics of harmony. So it is not remarkable that he had the same appreciation for music as most of the people he grew up with. But he had a catholic taste. He could get real enjoyment out of a Beethoven sonata or a Liszt rhapsody, but that didn't cut down his interest in the vanishing folk tunes of northern Indiana.

The early settlers must have brought a large repertoire of topical ballads to Ligonier . . . . the chants of bargemen . . . . old cradlesongs . . . . long and amusing recitatives about the deeds of forgotten colonial heroes . . . . localized versions of the history of the ubiquitous "Barbary Allen" and the "Old Lord Who Lived by the Northern Sea." Odd fragments out of this song bag were still to be heard in isolated hamlets of the neighborhood, though the echoes were fast dying away. Somehow young Pete found time to ferret out the forgotten minstrels. He listened to the peculiar melodies, he memorized the archaic and sometimes meaningless words and stored them away in his head alongside the operatic arias and the symphonic classics that among the hep cats of Ligonier were the jazz and jive of his day.

His inquisitive interest in this fossil culture seems never to have left him. Years later, when as the harassed wartime Governor of Illinois, he had virtually forgotten how to sleep, he found occasional relaxation in salons the like of which probably had never been held before in any governor's mansion in the United States. Bored by the exacting protocol of official receptions and similar specified functions, he began to organize little soirees that never got into the society columns. In steadily increasing numbers the forgotten men of the administration began to receive his invitation to dinner. These affairs, in the days of red and blue tickets, were something less than state banquets. The guest lists were unlike anything a social secretary had ever before been called upon to compile — country lawyers, farmers from the hinterlands — most of them shy men who in an entire term might never introduce a bill or take part in a debate or so much as raise their voices except to cast a vote.

Generally they were strangers to one another from districts and environments with widely divergent interests. But they had one thing in common. They were all skilled exponents of the state's neglected balladry.

So, after dinner, they would gather about the piano in the music room and sing of "One-Eyed Riley," "Raftsman Jim," "The Young Man Who Wouldn't Hoe Corn," and other interesting characters, far into the night. The governor, who can still get enthusiastic about a Bach concerto or a Schubert serenade, played the accompaniments, joined in lyrics he had heard before, and listened with an expert's enthusiasm to those that were new to him. Inevitably he had a very fine time. In music as in most other things he is an individualist.

His high-school career, which occupied his last years in the old home town, was uneventful or at any rate was no more eventful than his early childhood. He no longer rang fire bells, but he never went into retirement. His oldest friends and severest critics who frequent the meetings of Will Sack's hot-stove league admit that he continued to enjoy enough popularity to be greeted cheerfully by everybody in town, even though he had lost some of his glamour as a public nuisance.

So far as his old teachers remember, he doesn't seem to have been anything like a bookish student — perhaps not even diligent — but his remarkable memory made him a good one. He was a leader in all the school's extra curricular affairs and in four years of promoting athletic meets, concerts, interscholastic debates, and what not he acquired a considerable reputation as an organizer. He was interested in the glee club and the dramatic society and gave creditable performances in the school plays. He looked on the oratorical society with mixed emotions. He took advantage of the opportunity it gave him to learn how to think on his feet and to express himself extemporaneously. But the debates bored him stiff. The subjects so learnedly argued by his earnest young colleagues and himself were mostly political — and in politics he had no interest whatever.

Athletics came in for much of his attention during his high-school years. He played a fair game of basketball, and speed compensated for a lack of weight to make him a good quarterback. After his fifteenth birthday his mother never heard him mention any ambition to find a place in the big leagues, but his baseball steadily improved until even the local wiseacres granted that he might have prospects for a professional success.

At seventeen, however, he had abandoned the notion. Roy D. Keehn, a close friend of the family, had gone forth from Ligonier and was becoming famous as one of the foremost lawyers in Chicago. Young Pete, who had followed the newspaper reports of his career diligently, was impressed.

"Lawyers seem to do better than baseball players," he observed to his friend and teammate Herman Sack. "A lawyer is still pretty good when he's sixty-five. A big league player is generally through at forty — I guess maybe I'll be a lawyer."

A year later his mind was definitely made up, and he never changed it. He had never been in a courtroom, he had never heard of a man named Blackstone, and of course he hadn't the remotest inkling of a destiny that was being cooked up for him in Brooklyn. In that far bailiwick, to which the school geography referred as "the city of homes and churches," a somewhat dim-witted problem child was approaching manhood over a devious path. The record of this lad's boyhood is not so well documented as that of Pete Green. But something of it may be reconstructed from the tons of newspaper clippings which annotate the story of his effect on midwestern government and society. So vivid a character did he become in his adult years that those who knew him felt that he had been with them always. It is no trick at all to imagine him as he was on that fateful day when Dwight Green announced that he was going to study law. One can almost see him standing before his mother to make a similar declaration of intent:

"I'm going to be a hoodlum. I'm going to put murder on a business basis. I'm going to run Chicago ragged and I'm going to make millions of dollars. . . . ."

Dwight Green at that time had never heard of Alphonse Capone. On the other hand Alphonse Capone had never heard of Dwight Green — the misfortune appears to have been Capone's.

By the turn of the century a steadily expanding business had made life much easier for Dwight Green's father and uncles. Henry Green's principles of trade, which seem to have derived from the copybook maxims about frugality, honesty, and hard work, had paid out.

The original meat shop still counted a sizeable annual profit from local patronage. Fred Green's side venture in dairying was flourishing — so was a partnership of all three brothers in the brokerage of farm real estate. But the most profitable of their joint undertakings was a trade in live-stock with the Chicago and eastern markets — a holdover from the days of the big boom. This phase of their business under the principal direction of Dwight's father, Harry, who remained active in it until his death, by 1900 had made the Green brothers comfortably well off, if not wealthy. All of the children were assured of the college educations that their Grandfather Henry had planned for them. In family conference it was decided that John's Helen would go to Western College, Harry's Dwight to Wabash, and Fred's Will to the University of Wisconsin. By the time these eldest were of college age the financing of higher education for the younger ones was no longer enough of a problem to require a fraternal caucus.

Old Henry died at the age of sixty-seven in 1900 and was given a funeral befitting a pioneer whose unobtrusive works had affected the destiny of virtually the whole town. He had been ill for several years and during the last twelve months of his life seldom visited the enterprises that he and his sons had founded. His retail meat market was sold. Even before his death the cattle and farm brokerage businesses had been reorganized to supply the management that he was no longer able to give. But it is significant that so far as his family was concerned he seems never to have died at all.

So long as one of his sons remained in business in Ligonier, Henry Green was in the business also. His impress was on it. His basic methods of operation were unchanged. His wise advice was always available in times of crisis because he had given it long before he was laid in his grave.

Any old-timer in Ligonier will echo Will Sack's estimate of his influence:

"Henry made a closed corporation out of the Green family. They never forgot the things he taught them, and they never needed any help from the outside."

The curriculum of Henry Green's school was simple. His business was not his own but his family's. Within certain limitations it was a co-operative affair. It must be made to provide a living and a good living for his boys and their wives and their children. Its growing profits must be divided equally. But each beneficiary of this arrangement must pay his share in unremitting labor.

Fred, John Henry, and Harry each in turn took his place in the shop as apprentices, became expert butchers, and continued to work tirelessly at their trade well into adult life. Henry loved these lads. But he had a patriarchal sense of justice, and in his policy of equal returns for equal toil he never once made the way more easy for one than for the others.

Fred and John got only grammar school educations. Harry, as recorded, attended the new high school. But that made no difference insofar as his duty to the family enterprise was concerned. After the dismissal of his last class each day he would run — not walk — to the butcher shop, pile his books in a corner, don his white apron, and get on with his apprenticeship.

When he had completed his training as a meat cutter, he took his turn in the service of Henry's associated businesses, doing his bit on the Green farm, buying and selling livestock, and driving cattle to town for slaughter or shipment.

The financial policy of the meat shop was just as typical as it was novel. John Henry kept the books — an assignment which eventually took up most of his time. But in the beginning, accounting was an extremely minor feature of the Green business. There was no cash register in the market — nor any safe. All of the receipts were kept in a wooden drawer under the counter until (about three times a week) they were taken to Simon Straus's State Bank.

As each of the boys came to manhood — an age which Henry arbitrarily fixed at seventeen years — he was given a key to the till and free access to the cash. Out of the money on hand all of them would take what they needed for private expenses and the operation of their homes, leaving a sort of formless receipt:

"I got $10.35 — May 30 — John." "Eight Dollars — June — Harry." "Received $25 — July 3 — Henry Green."

These slips were collected and kept by John Henry. At specified times they were checked and totaled, and the largest total established as a standard for a distribution of funds. If the father or any of the sons had taken out less than this amount, they were paid in cash enough to make

Young Dwight Green set his sights on professional baseball, but soon decided that lawyers outlast ballplayers. He hauled lumber as body-building preparation for football.

Interrupting his college days to enlist as an infantryman in World War I, Dwight Green was transferred to the army air service, in which he earned a commission.

up the difference between their total withdrawals and the largest. Thus each of the four received a like amount. The residue, usually healthy, went into the bank.

By the time Harry had been taken into the firm and given his key to the cash drawer, cattle dealing had become the most important feature of the business. With its expansion there came problems of financing that Henry Green had never contemplated when he established his odd bookkeeping system.

There was, for instance, the galling instability of markets, and there were other incomprehensible headaches known as fluctuating customer credits and demand notes. The Greens for the first time began to find out about the long hiatuses between shipment and payment, the worrisome money shortage that so frequently lies between cash purchase and credit delivery. It was one of these recurrent difficulties that brought the concern into a new and entirely unfamiliar field.

The Green brothers made up their minds that the days of haphazard financing must end, that never must their business be jeopardized by lack of a place to turn for ready cash amply secured. They canvassed the county and by popular subscription raised enough capital to found a bank of their own. On March 1, 1906, the Farmers' and Merchants' Trust Company opened its doors in a building once occupied by the Green Brothers Meat Market, with Fred Green as president.

The Greens may not have known much about banking, but they had learned quite a lot about merchandising. The voice of Old Henry was still echoing among the tellers' cages in the former meat market as it had in the days when he was standing behind the meat block in the corner where Fred Green now sat at his desk as a bank president:

"To get along in any business you've got to give the customers something more or something better than they can get from your competition."

The aphorism seemed just as true in banking as in any other business. The new bank jarred its competitor on opening day with the announcement that it was prepared to pay three per cent interest on commercial deposits.

Such a thing was unheard of in Ligonier. A loan might cost as much as eighteen per cent and frequently did. But never since the first money lender set up shop in northern Indiana had anybody ever been paid a cent of interest on such deposits.

The Green's banking competitor openly denounced the policy of the Farmers' and Merchants' Trust as bad banking and suicidal business. But that didn't prevent the other bank's announcement next day that it would pay four per cent on deposits. The Green brothers promptly met this offer and there the competition ended.

So, among the influences that shaped the early career of Dwight Green, there was the new family interest in banking. Mathematics had always been one of his best subjects in school, and the routine arithmetic of accounting was never the puzzle to him that it must have been to his grandfather and uncles. Unconsciously he absorbed the lore of the currency markets — and credits and balances and interest. He couldn't escape conversations about bankruptcies and concealed assets. About the time young Alphonse Capone was beginning to be looked upon as a nuisance by saloonkeepers around the Five Points, Pete Green was able to make sense out of a bank statement. And while he never had much practical experience in the art, he somehow acquired a fair working knowledge of the basic systems of bookkeeping. Up in Chicago a smart financier named Samuel Insull was starting to build a vast network of public utilities girt round with the most complicated array of interlocking directorates and auditing departments the world had ever seen. But the name of Insull was probably just as strange to Pete Green as that of Capone.

He listened to the table conversations of his elders and showed polite but dispassionate interest in such remote affairs as $100,000 loans, million-dollar bond issues, liens, mortgages, and taxes. In vacation time and after school hours he contrived to earn a few more tangible dollars peddling the Chicago papers, driving cattle for his father and uncles, selling schoolbooks in Hugh Hutchinson's store, and jerking sodas for Sam Williams. He had heard in those days that "life is real, life is earnest." But that was somebody else's life.

6

CAME THE WAR

THERE WERE NO THRONGS OF WEEPING CITIZENRY at the Ligonier railroad station in 1915 when Dwight Green left to begin his freshman year at Wabash College. Going away to school seemed to be the least unusual thing that Harry Green's precocious young son had ever done. Other lads and girls of Ligonier had gone away to school — hundreds of them. You hardly realized it before they were back again. Pete wasn't breaking any home ties. He'd be home again in June and in other Junes to come, until finally he brought back his diploma and settled down to business with Green Brothers or in the Farmers' and Merchants' Trust.

What nobody, including Dwight himself, realized was that he was going for good. He wasn't coming back to the calm, happy life of the white house on Main Street nor to take a part in the pleasant life of Ligonier. Probably no faring adolescent before him had ever looked less like a

St. George getting ready to tangle with the dragon. But one sees a lot, and in different perspective, when one looks back from the far end of the road. Young Mr. Green was definitely on his way.

He spent the summer months immediately after his graduation from high school helping his father in the live-stock business and on the farm with as much diligence and patience as could be expected from a boy who was eagerly awaiting the opening of college in September and dreaming of quarterbacking the football team.

His consuming hope of winning a place on the team gave purpose to the heavy work on the farm which tough-ened his young muscles and gave greater endurance to his still developing body. And all the work he did that summer was also given purpose by his father's arrangement to pay his tuition and incidental expenses at college.

Young Dwight had saved a few hundred dollars out of his income from sparetime jobs of his boyhood so, with the help that his father gave him, going off to college pre-sented no pressing financial problem to the boy or his family. He had saved the money because he had been reared under the example of saving — of good living but living within income; the kind of working and living that at each year's end saw a little more accumulated than the year before. It was domestic and business economic doctrine with all the Greens that expenditures must always be kept within income. Something more than a quarter of a century later this Green family trait of character kept the State of Illinois solvent when, as Governor, Dwight H. Green resisted repeated attempts to spend the State's money recklessly. Pleasantly but firmly he insisted that the State live within its income. Those who had known him as always affable and gracious and always eager to adjust himself to another person's reasonable point of view, encountered the hard rock of Dwight Green's stubbornness when they tried to enlist him to mortgage the State's future by altering his policy of never spending more money than was coming in.

The freshman was eighteen years old when he reported at Wabash, considerably younger than other aspirants for places on the football squad. Part of his dream came true that year when he won a place on the team as substitute quarterback. As a second baseman he still liked to pull down a liner headed for right field and double a man off first, and he still enjoyed playing forward in basketball, but his athletic dream was still to be first string quarterback of the Little Giants. So at the end of his freshman year he did not return to Ligonier. To make his dream come true by strengthening his young body and in keeping with the Green trait of always earning more than you spend, he spent his first college summer vacation in Indianapolis driving a truck for a lumber company.

"The varsity quarterback was graduated that June," he recalls, "and I wanted to take his place on the team. I thought I'd better do something that would keep me toughened up, and then there was the matter of revenue to pay my way at the parties and dances and all the other things we did when we went out to have fun. It was the right kind of job for both purposes. I used to deliver 2,000 feet of lumber from the truck and 2,500 feet from the trailer. I had some help at the yard loading the stuff, but when I took it off I was on my own."

Came the War

Dwight Green went back to Wabash to become quarterback of the Little Giants in his sophomore year. The big game with DePauw was played in Indianapolis. Pete Green was the shortest player on the Wabash football team, but was an accurate passer. There was a play in which Quarterback Green sent a short pass over center, short but high, so high that of the twenty-two men on the field only two of the Little Giants — towering giants who played football and basketball — could reach the ball. Quarterback Green used this play many times in the big game. Final score: Wabash 26, DePauw 13. That may have been his peak attainment as an athlete, at any rate it ended his ambition to star in competitive sports. But his recollection of it is modest.

"Of course," he says, "I only got to be first-string quarterback after the varsity quarterback was graduated." But Heze Clark wrote in the Indianapolis Times that "Green has the earmarks of a great field general."

Now, more than thirty years later, the importance that attaches to Dwight Green's college athletic career is that he was determined to become quarterback and he did; the career and his physical preparation for it gave him the endowment of a strong body that enables him to work as Governor and as the head of the Republican Party in Illinois with a vigor that astounds all of his associates and for long hours that exhaust most of them. He has kept his body in the kind of condition that enables him still to get out and play a pretty fair second base in the annual ball games between members of the Senate and House of the Illinois General Assembly. One way he keeps fit is by bowling a fair-to-middling game when he can find a few hours for recreation in the winter months. And when his duties permit him to take an afternoon off in summer he likes to tee off for eighteen holes of better-than-average duffer golf.

It would be nice to record that young Dwight Green studied as hard at Wabash as he worked to become first-string quarterback of the Little Giants. But who knows how hard a popular young collegian studies when he is interested in football, baseball, and basketball, in class fights and parties and dances, in those long midwinter night bull sessions with his fraternity brothers, when young men delude themselves that they are living in a man's world, and in those all too short springtime dates with girls.

Pete Green made fair-to-good reason in college and he never forgot what was the essential reason for his presence at Wabash — to obtain an education. Nowadays, as a member of the Wabash board of trustees, he gives similar weight to college activities and the essential purpose of the college.

When he enrolled, he selected a liberal arts course with the object of specializing in the law. He had an increasing interest in economics. And to this day, when he mentions Rollo Brown, who taught English at Wabash and wrote short stories, he speaks of him with the respectful affection a young collegian has for a professor whose classes he enjoys, to whose precepts he gives attentive ear, and whose example he accepts as a pattern for gracious and intelligent living.

He had a girl, of course. When she and her girl friends came to Wabash — a men's college — for the fall, winter, or spring dance and week-end party, they stayed in the fraternity house, and Dwight and the other boys who lived in the Kappa Sigma house would find places to stay in

Crawfordsville. It was all in the gentle pattern of pre-World War I American college life.

Twenty-seven years later, in 1944, Dwight Green could not remember all the details of events at the Kappa Sigma house, but Kappa Sigma remembered Dwight Green, for whom life by this time was indeed real and earnest. The fraternity selected him for its annual "man-of-the-year" award. "Some may equal but none excel," read the inscription. When one of his elders who had known him in the days of his Ligonier childhood read this, he smiled and muttered something about turning out the fire department.

When Wabash College opened its doors in September, 1917, Dwight Green was not there. He was really concerned with a fire — a world in the blaze of war. Within a month after school had closed for the summer, he had enlisted at Indianapolis, where he was putting in his second season for the lumber company, and made application for service in the air corps. He was then aged 20.

While the world blazed fiercely Dwight Green hauled lumber until September, because an American army unprepared for overnight expansion did not call him up for service until then. He was assigned to the infantry and good-naturedly endured the broad-humored hazing which is the lot of all rookies, but which was pretty easy going to Private Green after the indignities that are heaped upon college freshmen and the rough going of fraternity initiation. A month later he was delighted by transfer to the air corps.

The history of his army career is like that of most of the lads who aspired to pilot the flying coffins of the First World War. He spent two months at a ground school at the University of Illinois, was graduated, and was transferred with his squadron to a sort of preflight school at Camp Dick, Dallas, Texas.

Camp Dick at the time was a sort of concentration point from which the prospective pilots were sent out to flying fields in small batches. Then, as in another war, the army had plenty of would-be flyers but faced a direful lack of planes and instructors. When Dwight Green arrived the camp had become a bottleneck, with fresh squadrons arriving nearly every day and only a few men going anywhere else.

Eventually transfer from this roaring melee to a flying field was placed on a competitive basis. The squadron that made the best showing in drill got the best grading and the squadron with the best grades over a given period was given priority on the transfer list. Green's squadron was released in ten days and he was sent to Kelly Field, San Antonio, for preliminary training.

He learned to fly in the old Jenny (Curtiss JN4D), a single-motored training plane. The time was little more than a dozen years after the Wright brothers had first flown a few feet at Kitty Hawk. When Officer Candidate Green and his instructor went up in the Jenny they had no means of verbal communication. They devised hand signals. If the pupil had his right wing down too much, a motion of the instructor's hands told him so. A touch of the left or right ear indicated too much rudder one way or another.

Day after day instructor and pupil flew the same course, and each day the officer candidate was permitted to handle the controls a little more. At a fork in a creek they made a left turn, at a red barn they made another left turn, and so it went until young Green had four and one-half hours in the air.

"Do you think you can fly alone?" asked the instructor.

"Sure," replied the pupil, forgetting his military manners in this great moment.

"Well, go ahead and see what you can do."

So young Mr. Green soloed. But after all these years he still says, "If they had ever moved that red barn I'd still be going." As Governor he does most of his traveling by plane. But those who accompany him on these trips, hopeful of bringing their pet projects to his attention, find little time for conversation. Mr. Green is up ahead with the pilot, "flying" the ship.

The second time Dwight Green flew alone was the last time he flew for a while. The observation tower on the primary solo field was filled with officers. A strong wind was blowing and quite a few planes were in the air as the young flyer was about to take off crosswind. At that moment a checkered flag signaled a change in the line of take-off and landing.

"I gave her the gun," he recalls, "and headed toward the observation tower. I was confident I would clear it easily but the officers didn't share my confidence. As I went over the top with plenty of daylight between the tower and my ship, the officers were scramming, running down the stairs as fast as they could go. After I had put the ship down I was told I was wanted in the tower. The lieutenant bawled me out and benched me for a week."

After a week on the bench, the youthful cadet was back in the air. It was not long, however, before he was grounded in a hospital bed. In early April, 1918, flying a ship of different design from the one used in primary training, he cracked up. His injuries were not serious, although he was in base hospital for three weeks and out of flying for a month. He had a numb leg for a long time and carries facial scars — mementoes of his dive through the cowling — to this day.

Candidate Green survived these misadventures to fly again — and to be commissioned on May 31, 1918. He was transferred to Brooks Field, also at San Antonio, to enter the new instructors' school where the "Gosport System," a British training technique, was taught. When he had completed the course, he was transferred to Mather Field, Sacramento, California, as an instructor. He remained there until the finish of the war.

Dwight Green wasn't bothered much by the postwar problems that plagued so many of the men mustered out of the First World War. He knew what he wanted to do and how to go about doing it, and facilities were close at hand.

As soon as he got his discharge, he matriculated at Leland Stanford University because it was the nearest school of any he cared to attend. He was given two years' college credits for his stay at Wabash and a third of a year for his work in the army. He took the usual college subjects plus a course in "Introductory Law." Baseball also claimed his attention, but he tore a ligament in his left knee shortly after he got into uniform and was on crutches most of the time until he left Stanford at the end of June, 1919.

In July he came to Chicago to ask advice from Roy D. Keehn and remained as a clerk in Keehn's law office. Thus far his life since leaving Ligonier had been varied enough, though there had been little in it to give a hint of the pattern of things to come. He was still a boy, scarcely out of his teens, when he came in bashfully to consult with Keehn about his future. His army service had given him some poise and assurance. He had a pleasant personality and a lot of his mother's even disposition, plus plenty of his grandfather's persistence. He had convinced himself that he wanted to be a lawyer and, being what he was, there was little likelihood that he might change his mind. But he was still beset by uncertainties. He was still fond of baseball. He liked flying and, young as he was, foresaw a day when aviation would present a field of almost unlimited opportunity. He was fascinated by the newspaper business in which he was presently to achieve eminence as one of the most-fired reporters in the history of journalism.

The law, he was beginning to find out, was more complicated than he had been led to suspect. It was full of specialties and specialists and there must have been times when he felt hopeless and baffled at the thought of choosing a particular branch of it as a life work.

But if Dwight Green, through an excusable lack of omniscience, was overlooking a few opportunities to fit himself for an important place in the life he was just entering, there were compensations. The world with which he was so little acquainted was obligingly setting his stage for him. Prohibition had come into the land. The income tax was beginning to take rank as one of the government's foremost industries. A new class of malefactors was coming into being. And whether he liked it that way or not, young Pete Green's career was going to be pretty well marked out by the time he had qualified for his diploma as a lawyer.

He had wished to go back to Stanford, but Keehn persuaded him to enter the University of Chicago. It was a wise choice. In Keehn's office he had an opportunity to learn the mechanics of the law while going on with his schooling. And the Law School of the University of Chicago had a faculty of such experts as Dean Hall on constitutional law and torts, Judge Hinton on evidence, Mechem on partnership and agency. Woodward on the law of equity and trust, Freund on administrative law, Bigelow on real and personal property law, and Puttkammer on criminal law. The Law School faculty was at that time rated one of the best in the country.

Roy Keehn in 1919 was counsel for the Hearst newspapers in Chicago; through his influence young Dwight became campus correspondent for the Examiner at the University. He did well enough during his first year to get a vacation job as a cub reporter on the same newspaper and so came to establish an unusual record.

7

COLOSIMO, TORRIO, AND AL BROWN

THE CHICAGO THAT YOUNG DWIGHT REDISCOVERED in the fall of 1919 had changed a lot from the day when a starry-eyed boy from Ligonier, looking at it from the right-field bleachers in old Cub's Park on the West Side, had considered it the capital of all the world. If he had taken time to analyze the situation, it must have seemed to him the most unlikely field for the exemplification of law and justice inasmuch as it was well on its way toward achieving an international reputation for classic lawlessness. Prohibition was only a few months old when, with Roy D. Keehn, he attempted to plan a future that was already being plotted for him in the vicinity of Wabash Avenue and Twenty-second Street. But recooked alcohol, needled beer, and bathtub gin had already been invented, and bootlegging was beginning to take stature as a major industry.

The outward signs of what was to come may not have been manifest to a youthful ex-aviator busy with personal concerns and filled with lofty ideals. A long and vicious crime wave that lacked only corpses to make it the equal of any plague to be contrived by the gang commandos had come to an end. Wise heads in the police department and the newspaper offices were under no illusions about what had happened to it. The streets were safe for homing pedestrians at night merely because the pickpockets, morons, and stick-up men were finding better pay for shorter hours in the business of hooch distribution. Crime hadn't left the community. It had merely tricked itself out in snap-brimmed hats, belted coats with pointed shoulders, and pearl-gray spats. And it had changed its address from slum flophouses to a lot of reasonably re-spectable hotels. But Dwight Green probably didn't know that.

Looking back over the newspapers of the period one gets the idea that most of the citizens of Chicago were content to take the blessings of sudden peace with unin-quiring gratitude. The average householder who for the first time in many months found it more convenient — and just as safe — to carry his money in his pocket instead of in his shoes found no reason to study the city's sudden reformation. Experience may have taught him to expect no permanence in virtue. But in the meantime life had be-come more or less pleasant. Robberies were so infrequent that editors once more began to look upon them as print-able news. There was one night when not a single major crime found its way onto the police ticker, and there

are men alive today who remember this era as Chicago's
golden age.

Thus Dwight Green's first months as a clerk in Keehn's
law office did not differ much from those he had known
in Ligonier. He met pleasant people. All about him were
interesting things, and his work wasn't so arduous that he
lacked leisure to enjoy them. Some homey philosopher
has said that "what you don't know doesn't hurt you."
In young Mr. Green's case it turned out to be a sage
observation.

Green found lodgings out near the University of Chicago
early in August, 1919. It is an interesting, if not significant,
coincidence that on virtually the same day young Alphonse
Capone got off a train in the LaSalle Street Station and
reported to one John Torrio in a South Side flat. Green
and Capone had been born in the same year and, according to legend still circulated in Little Sicily, narrowly
escaped sharing the same birthday. If you want further
evidence of the odd workings of chance, both carried
facial scars, Green's (now almost unnoticeable) the results of his crack-up in an army plane, Capone's (which
looked like a memento of Old Heidelberg) the handiwork
of some forgotten carver in a New York dive.

When you go into the early history of Capone you
find few credible records. The pasts of dictators and other
big bugaboos have a way of altering to fit in with later
accomplishments. Young Capone seems to have been born
in Italy of respectable parents who brought him at an
early age to Brooklyn. Less capable of proof is the story
that the neighbors considered him a boy of very fine

character and great charm. During his adolescence he
never got into trouble with the police which, considering
his so-called public life, is not remarkable. Come to think
about it his contacts with the authorities in Chicago were
purely social until he stepped into Judge Wilkerson's
court on his way to Alcatraz.

There is some evidence to show that not all of his
family shared his virtuous attitude. His brother Frank
made more or less of a career out of membership in the
Five Points Gang across the river and came to be the close
associate of a shrewd, well-mannered leader — the same
Torrio to whom Alphonse, the one-time model youth,
reported on his arrival in Chicago.

Legend bridges the interval between the time when
"that nice young Capone boy" got tired of setting a good
example for his neighborhood in Brooklyn and the day he
embarked on a new career as Torrio's henchman. In the
newspaper files you can find the story that he got into a
brawl in a saloon and assaulted a customer, who flopped
to the floor, apparently dead but mostly drunk. Errone-
ously informed that the police were looking for him on
a murder charge, he made a quick trip over the bridge
to find refuge with his brother Frank. Thus, it is explained,
he came to join the Five Points Gang and train himself
for a new life.

Crime of some varieties had become big business in
Chicago even before the enactment of the Eighteenth
Amendment. Gambling, for instance, had become so well
organized that it was the virtual monopoly of a few men
who had developed the market with the imprimatur of
the City Hall and the well-paid neutrality of the police.

The brothel keepers had a sort of loose federation for the promotion of business and mutual protection. The system of business direction later to be known as "The Racket" had not progressed very far, but most of its essential features were well enough known in the community to be commonplace. Dynamiting and murder as methods for settling jurisdictional disputes outside the law had filled fat files in the offices of the Crime Commission. The professional killer wasn't any more of a novelty in Chicago at the turn of the century than he had been in the Venice of the Doges. Where an illegal stake was sufficient to warrant assassination you could always hire an assassin, and so far as available records show, the price was not very high. That there had been no unusual chronicle of sudden death during the first days of prohibition would seem to mean only that it takes a little time to develop a new industry even when there is plenty of experienced help.

Big Jim Colosimo, whose ostensible business was the operation of a restaurant — and a pretty good one — in Wabash Avenue on the edge of the old levee district, knew all about the ramifications of extralegal business. He had numerous interests aside from the serving of spaghetti dinners — wine included — at fifty cents a plate. He had an interest in a string of brothels that were not supposed to exist. And, it is hardly necessary to mention, he had unusually strong political connections.

He was a humorous, affable man whose booming laugh might have been taken to indicate an easy conscience. His activities in vice were part of what one might call his private life. They left no outward mark on him. He had hundreds — perhaps thousands — of friends who considered his business success the just reward of honesty, hard work, and pleasant manners.

Colosimo was aware, no doubt, of what people thought of him. But he was too old a hand in corruption to think for a minute that this good opinion was unanimous. His income from the women of his neighborhood was a very tidy sum indeed and, although the term "muscling in" had not yet been invented, he knew something of the process such words would so graphically describe. He knew that man is by nature envious, and the richer he got the more he wondered how long other fortune seekers were going to let him live to enjoy his prosperity.

In this situation he sent for John Torrio — a boyhood companion and trusted friend. Torrio became ostensibly a sort of overseer for Colosimo's properties in the forgotten levee district. Actually he was Big Jim's bodyguard and constant shadow.

The choice in many ways was good. Torrio was intelligent — in comparison with the average I.Q. of the gangsters of his time, his rating would have made him look something like an Einstein. He was suave, diplomatic, cool-headed. Furthermore he was tough — as he must have been to rise to prominence at the Five Points. But as a bodyguard he had one defect. He didn't like to kill people — not in person. Battle in ambush had no appeal to him. The situation became acute when he realized that because of his open association with Colosimo, he was likely to become a target on his own account.

So he sent for his protege, Al Capone, to take over this important phase of his employment. And thus Capone began his career in the city in which he was to achieve the coveted position of Public Enemy Number One as bodyguard to a bodyguard.

Like Dwight Green, young Al Brown, as he was known to his associates, put in a few months marking time. Prohibition had come and Colosimo, thanks to his efficient organization and his entree to the City Hall and his acquaintanceship with every thug in the First Ward, found himself in a fine position to take advantage of it. The First Ward wasn't all of Chicago by any means, but it took in the business section — the Loop — and was de facto the wealthiest, and therefore the most important, district in town. Colosimo may not have been the city's first bootlegger, but he was the first to see the advantages of wholesale operation; with his ready-made prestige and backing he might well have become the John D. Rockefeller of the illicit alcohol trade from one end of Cook County to the other.

But for all his foresight and for all the assistance he got from eager politicians who shared his vision of unparalleled wealth, he experienced the misfortunes that so often spoil the careers of hard-working pioneers.

One morning in May, 1920, before the sleepy waiters had come in to set the tables for the blue-plate lunch, some incompletely identified friend walked into his office and shot him dead.

Dwight Green, like everybody else in Chicago, took a deep interest in the newspaper accounts of what the police were calling an unexplainable mystery. But like everybody else he saw no deep significance in the murder. He had been in Colosimo's once or twice for luncheon. And if he had any remote idea that Big Jim's murder might have an effect on the social life, politics, and morals of Chicago for a whole decade, it was not on account of the dead man's rumored connection with the market for handmade gin. Instead he breathed a sigh in reminiscence and wondered if Colosimo's successor would continue to put out spaghetti dinners of the same quality for the same price.

8

RISE OF THE HOODLUMS

Not until long afterward was the murder of Jim Colosimo ascribed officially to rivalry in the alcohol trade. Chicago still remembered an era of terrorism spread by offshoots of the Mafia and independent extortionists lumped together in the crime stories as "the black hand." Colosimo's Italian derivations made it seem for a time as if he might have been the belated victim of one of the old gangs. But in all respects save for error in the establishment of motive, his removal established a pattern from which there was to be little or no deviation in hundreds of killings in the years to come.

There were no witnesses — or at least none came forward. The dead man's books revealed no sources of income other than his restaurant. It was an open secret that he had been financially interested in numerous brothels that could be found by everybody but the city authorities within a few blocks of his office. But, of course, nobody knew anything about that. As the press so repetitively put it, the police were "baffled." And they remained baffled until the repeal of the Eighteenth Amendment. Nobody was charged with the crime, and naturally nobody was punished for it.

Late in life Colosimo had married Dale Winter, a singer in his cabaret. Remembering that, detectives assigned to the case hinted darkly that jealousy is always a good motive for murder. So the wife he had divorced was brought in for a questioning that even at the time seemed too silly to merit more than a few paragraphs in the news. One of the newspapers learned through a tipster that one Frank Yale (spelled U-a-l-e), a Brooklyn gunman who was also, and appropriately enough, an undertaker, had come to Chicago to see Colosimo the day before his death. But so far as there is any record of the matter, nobody ever questioned Uale. He went on filling his own coffins, virtually unmolested, until, long after Big Jim was forgotten, somebody blasted him off his own front steps.

Colosimo's funeral was another event that set a mode. Other big shots such as Dion O'Banion and Hymie Weiss were to be laid away with more ornate obsequies. But Colosimo's was the first of its sort in Chicago, and as a gaudy spectacle of public grief it had few precedents anywhere in the world. About five thousand mourners turned out for it. "Among the honorary pallbearers," says the Crime Commission's report of the spectacle, "were aldermen, judges, congressmen, noted singers of the Chicago Opera Company, leaders of his immigrant group, and his associates in underworld activities. Less distinguished in the assemblage were fat "madams" from his bereft brothels and scores of the sorrow-stricken girls who had contributed to his support.

Maybe the city's best people hadn't talked much about Big Jim's position as overlord of the old levee district, but nobody who read the newspapers, even occasionally, could have been ignorant of the fact. Chicago was exhibiting a strange morality in those days. The populace, especially that part of it which held public office, found it easy to forgive the sins of the dead, even in the case of a super pander, and to sympathize with any picturesque black-guard cut down before he had had a chance to spend his blood money. The town, if one may draw any conclusion at all from the files of the daily press of 1919 and 1920, was complacent, apathetic, and demoralized — ethically prepared for such a dictatorship as that of Al Capone, although at that time the young man from Brooklyn was principally employed as a bouncer in "The Four Deuces," a dive at 2222 South Wabash Avenue.

A thousand members of the First Ward Democratic Club were at the head of Colosimo's cortege under the personal leadership of Alderman "Bathhouse John" Coughlin and Michael "Hinky-Dink" Kenna. Big Jim had been denied the last rites of the Catholic Church, but Alderman Coughlin met this situation by kneeling at the foot of the coffin and reciting prayers for the dead. The procession, after leaving Colosimo's home, wound through the district that had known him for so many years. In front of his restaurant the hearse was stopped for ten minutes to give the mourners, including the judges and other notables, a period of silent meditation. Then the body was taken out to the cemetery and reverently interred.

There was no fanfare about the disposal of Colosimo's unlisted properties. No mention of his successor in the control of the unrecognized levee or the growing liquor industry got into the newspapers — not just then. But there has never been any dispute about what happened.

No matter who had brought about the death of Big Jim, no matter what ideas may have been in the heads of envious opportunists outside his organization, the business he had built up so painstakingly fell into the hands of the man he had virtually designated as his heir. John Torrio, with the blessing of Colosimo's anonymous backers, took over without competition — without argument — and immediately started upon an ambitious program of expansion.

Whatever else one may say about John Torrio, he was smarter than Colosimo ever had been. He established his intelligence beyond dispute by coming through the prohibition period alive. He had the diplomacy as well as the wiles to carry out Colosimo's half-formed plans for a monopoly in the contraband liquor trade and, save for a couple of contretemps, might have become a dictator in his own right — a more powerful dictator than any of his rivals. But like most shrewd men he had his blind spots. This, he demonstrated by putting his trust in his old friend and protege, "Scarface Al" Brown, *nee* Capone.

"Scarface Al" achieved no notoriety as Torrio's principal lieutenant. Like his employer he believed in complete self-effacement. He moved in a mysterious way his wonders to perform, and his increased responsibilities and improved prospects made no outward change in his life. He was still, so far as casual acquaintances knew, the bouncer for the Four Deuces. In this capacity he was known slightly by an increasing number of police who thought him a minor tough of no particular consequence. He had no trouble with them, even while recruiting for Torrio one of the most talented collections of thugs ever turned loose on a supposedly civilized community.

Other ambitious hoodlums were rising up in areas beyond the old Colosimo jurisdiction, laying foundations for the trade rivalry that was to put three hundred and seventy-five gangsters in their graves between 1921 and 1926. But this was still the period of organization. Markets had not yet been well defined. And no beer or alcohol provider had as yet become important enough to merit assassination at the hands of his competitors.

All was quiet on the prohibition front during the rest of 1920 save for the cluttering of the municipal docket with the cases of speakeasy proprietors who had not yet learned the techniques of their new business. Chicago was still brawling and noisy but not much concerned about the future, open in its gambling, hypocritical about its other vices, plagued by graft, and badly governed. But the gangsters had not yet made any attempt to take it over. They apparently had not yet recognized their opportunity.

9

MR. HOWEY AND MR. CARSON

D WIGHT GREEN'S MODEST POSITION ON THE OLD *Chicago Examiner* gave him an exceptional chance to learn what was going on in this calm before chaos. Despite the evasions of public officials and the double talk of the police, there was nothing very secret about the progress of the great bootlegging enterprise. When a newspaperman discovered that synthetic liquor or a variety of beer might be had in any "coffee shop" and that "coffee shops" ran two to the average block, he didn't have to be told that there must be sources of supply and arrangements for delivery. Chattering retailers let drop the names of the salesmen who took their orders for gin. So it wasn't long before every city editor had compiled a sort of Who's Who of the alcohol trade and was sending out reporters to find out little things about the riffraff who promised to become tomorrow's millionaires. Young Green in the normal course of his job was given an education in the character and methods of gangsters that proved to be as valuable to him as anything he ever got out of a lawbook. He may be excused, however, if he failed to recognize his blessings.

The *Examiner* in 1920 and for some years afterward was the most unpromising training ground for a prospective public figure that anybody could well imagine. Walter Howey, the durable genius, was managing editor. Frank Carson, of unfading memory, was city editor. Dwight Green's own estimate of the pair is as good as any.

He recalled them vividly on the occasion of Carson's death as managing editor of the *Daily News* (New York).

"Brother!" he exclaimed with poignant nostalgia. "There was a combination! As a team they were the most terrific thing that had happened to Chicago since Mrs. O'Leary's cow kicked over the lamp. Really they were more important than the big fire because they lasted longer."

He came into association with these stalwarts without any formal introduction and spent most of his time during the first few weeks as a reporter trying to keep out of their way. Nobody had instructed him in the odd ways of the *Examiner* but then, as now, he had a talent for scenting trouble before it came close to him. And however slight his interest in the science of politics he had seen something of its mechanical workings in classrooms and army camps. Instinctively, in an organization where nearly everybody was gunning for everybody else, he plotted a good course.

His sponsor in journalism, Roy D. Keehn, stood high in the opinion of William Randolph Hearst; as a consequence he exercised a considerable control over the two local Hearst newspapers. It was natural that an individualist like Howey, who remembered Keehn chiefly as a somewhat brash campus correspondent at the University of Chicago, should take a dim view of his guidance. The pair were continuously at loggerheads.

In the circumstances, when Keehn set out to find a job for his young protege from Ligonier, he looked about for an ear more friendly than Howey's. He called up the news editor, Duffy Cornell, and Pete Green was slipped into a corner of the *Examiner's* local room unheralded and unnoticed. There was no great difficulty about it. The *Examiner* operated in a bedlam whose minor personnel was constantly changing. It is doubtful that even Carson knew the names of half of his staff. Everybody responded to the simple salutation, "Hey! You!" and the turmoil of the local room was so varied and so continuous that one probably could have smuggled an elephant into it without arousing comment from the city desk.

So, for a couple of weeks, the neophyte reporter got along pretty well. As another unidentified "Hey! You!" he got sundry little assignments that he was able to cover without instruction or criticism. Some of the things he wrote got into print, and every seven days an unquestioning cashier gave him $22. He began, after a while, to feel some security in his policy of self effacement. And then, of course, trouble caught up with him. He should have realized that anybody who contrived to stay on the payroll for more than five days was automatically an old-timer and a marked man.

One night as he sat at his typewriter putting together some information about a milk wagon that had been obliterated by a streetcar in Oak Park, he experienced the unpleasant sensation that somebody was looking over his shoulder. He turned around and found himself staring into the unamused face of Walter Howey.

"How long have you been working here?" Howey wanted to know.

"Two weeks," replied the future Governor of Illinois.

"You're fired," said Mr. Howey without bothering to go into unnecessary explanations. "You are fired as of right now."

So young Mr. Green left the palpitant reading public of Chicago in ignorance of what had happened to the milk wagon in Oak Park, got his coat, and made the first of his numerous exits from the newspaper business.

In a few days he was back again, of course. Roy Keehn was a man of considerable tenacity and resourcefulness. Young Mr. Green got a chance to write other bits about milk wagons for nearly another week before his discovery, this time by Carson. Once more he went out into the night.

That might have ended his journalistic career on any paper less spectacularly run than the *Examiner*. But the city desk was too preoccupied with its own concerns to give much attention to cubs — even cubs that it didn't want. So, with cheerful persistence, Pete Green, egged on by Keehn, came back again and again, like a commuter who had an unalterable date to catch the 5:15.

Carson, who had only a secondary interest in the feud that was promoting Mr. Green's instability, came, in time, to look on the whole performance as a sort of game. When, in some unusual lull in the customary riot, his restless eye would fall upon the now familiar figure in the back of the room, he never seemed to be disturbed. A pained look would come over his face and he would proceed with his part of the routine in pantomime. Without comment, without so much preliminary as a shouted "Hey! You!" he would crook his finger at his unwelcome reporter and point toward the door. Just as quietly and efficiently, Mr. Green would get his coat and retire. On those few occasions when Carson failed to notice "Roy Keehn's stooge" he would be reminded by his alert assistant, George (Ash) DeWitt, now Hearst's executive editor in Chicago.

Unfortunately there is no available record of how often this act was repeated. As Dwight Green remembers it, he was going out into Madison Street every four or five days. But there is no doubt about his unique record. It has remained unbroken, even in Chicago, for twenty-seven years.

It was a foregone conclusion that sooner or later this fantastic business would lose its novelty. One or the other — Howey, Carson, or Keehn — was certain to tire, and as it turned out, the Howey-Carson axis tired first. There came a time when Carson caught Green's eye and failed to gesture with the crooked finger and a day shortly thereafter when Howey greeted him gruffly in the elevator. By that time the young man from Ligonier had every right to consider himself a reporter. He was fired once more before he left the newspaper business for good. But that was for something else. Like the cub so frequently celebrated in the magazine stories, he got a scoop — in this instance a notable "picture scoop." But he didn't get any of the fictional rewards for it. Instead, he got the personal escort of Mr. Carson out of the office.

Mr. Howey and Mr. Carson

Dwight Green was getting toward the end of his second summer with the *Examiner* in August 5, 1921, when one Belton Kennedy was found shot to death in Beverly Glen on the outskirts of Los Angeles. The case attracted much attention in Chicago and particularly in the office of Walter Howey when Madalynne Obenchain, estranged wife of Ralph Obenchain of Evanston, was charged with the murder.

Madalynne, who had been a popular student at Northwestern University, was a young woman of more than ordinary beauty and charm and could not conceivably have had any reluctance about having her picture taken. When she went away from Chicago she had left dozens of friends scattered through the North Shore suburbs — all of them with snapshot albums and memory books. But when the diligent "art editors" turned loose their hordes of picture chasers to pick up a printable likeness of her, they discovered that such things were about as scarce as original portraits of Mona Lisa. Maybe Madalynne had been really camera-shy. Maybe her friends loved her too much to part with the treasured mementos that would have added to her unfortunate notoriety. But at any rate the most experienced searchers in the business canvassed the town and its environs from Waukegan to Gary without locating so much as a recognizable tintype of the lady who had been the toast of Evanston.

In this emergency the *Examiner* was no better off than any of its competitors, save that it had the genius of Frank Carson. He never revealed his sources of information and he never talked about how he did his tricks. But somehow he located a photograph of Madalynne Obenchain when everybody else had failed . . . . and a good one.

[73]

It was standing on an easel on a display table where hundreds of people were looking at it every day in the studio at the Edgewater Beach Hotel. There remained only the detail of sending a reporter out to get it — and it speaks well for Dwight Green's changed status in the organization that he was picked for the job.

Carson was matter-of-fact about it.

"You go out to the Edgewater Beach Hotel and get that photograph," he directed. And he gave elaborate details concerning what it looked like and just where to find it. "I don't care how you get it, but get it. If you come back without it you'll be fired — this time for keeps, Roy Keehn or no Roy Keehn."

"This is Sunday and the studio will be closed," mentioned young Mr. Green.

"What's that got to do with it?" inquired Mr. Carson.

So, with all the enthusiasm one might have expected to find in a modest youth suddenly called upon to work a first-class miracle, Mr. Green went out to the Edgewater Beach Hotel.

All the ground floor shops have two entrances, one from the street and another from an inner arcade. Through the show window on the arcade he speedily located the picture just as Carson had described it. It was barely six feet away. Save for the plate glass he could have had his hands on it in two steps. But the shop was empty and the doors were locked; so far as accessibility was concerned, Madalynne's lovely likeness might just as well have been in the middle of Lake Michigan.

He went to William Dewey, the manager of the hotel, and frankly explained his difficulty.

"We might find a pass key that would let you in there," Mr. Dewey conceded. "But of course I couldn't open that door without permission from the lady who owns the shop. I'll call her. I can't see why she shouldn't be willing to co-operate with you."

So he called the lady, who replied with an indignant outburst that could easily be heard three feet from the receiver.

"Under no circumstances will I give that picture to anybody," she declared. "I can't do anything for this reporter. And you will please tell him so. . . . ." And more to that effect.

Mr. Dewey, when he turned from the phone, was sympathetic but firm.

"You see how it is," he said. "I'm sorry I can't help you out. But she says no. And I guess her decision is final."

Young Mr. Green thanked him sadly and started down the stairs toward the street. Mr. Dewey wasn't looking when he turned into the arcade to take another look at the studio door. He tried the knob once more. The lock was just as firmly set as it had been when he tried it the first time. But he noticed one thing that had escaped him in his earlier inspection. The transom was open — a good eight inches.

Mr. Carson's emissary then explored the lower reaches of the hotel until he found an assistant janitor who thought that for two dollars he could find a stepladder. He did find one and carried it to the arcade, where a number of interested hotel guests watched Pete Green go into the studio over the top of the door. . . . .

Mr. Carson was pleased no end when the picture, neatly bordered with a three-dollar frame, was laid on his desk. He went so far as to jump up from his chair, clap his frequently fired reporter on the back, and tell him he was a real newspaperman who had done extremely well and was to be congratulated on his dependability — which, from Carson, was an unusual encomium.

In the morning Madalynne Obenchain was no longer the Invisible Woman. Every two-cent customer of the *Examiner* found that he had her wistful portrait for his very own to do with as he pleased. It was a clean beat and Carson had made the most of it — four columns on page one, surrounded by a lot of laudatory reading matter. Once it had been copied, he had wrapped it up with its frame and mailed it back to the studio, where it arrived almost as soon as the lady manager. This thoughtfulness, however, did little to forestall indignant outcries and threats of reprisal.

The studio owner threatened to sue Manager Dewey and his hotel. Mr. Dewey threatened to sue the *Examiner* and cancel his advertising. He stormed into Howey's office and demanded that something be done about the outrage immediately. The advertising manager pleaded. Mr. Howey cajoled. And in the midst of the confusion there entered the echoing local room a proud young reporter, prepared to accept the plaudits of his fellow workers. . . . . to wit, Mr. Green.

"You're fired," roared Mr. Carson. "We won't have men on the staff of the *Examiner* who refuse to live up to the rules."

"Yessir," replied the bewildered reporter, and he took the well-known trail toward the cashier's office, wondering what had happened to him.

Two days later he got a telephone call from Carson. "Sorry I couldn't make it earlier," was the message. "But anyway the heat's off and everybody's happy. Let's come back to work."

So Dwight Green returned to the *Examiner* local room for what was to be his farewell performance in journalism. His reappearance at his desk was notable in that it marked the end of what he had come to term his "rebounding mat act." He was never to be fired again, and Carson had given him some assurance that he might expect as much consideration as the city desk meted out to any other member of the staff. And that wasn't the end of the miracle. He found himself raised to the status of a graduate reporter. He began to get regular assignments — not very important ones, as he recalls them, but anyway assignments of the sort that he had never been trusted to cover as a raw cub. He got a chance to go out into the odd corners of the city and to write his own stories. And somebody else took over his thankless job of chasing pictures.

Like most newspaper alumni he is unable to recall the details of most of the bits of news that he gathered and furnished for the *Examiner's* circulation. None of them had any world-shaking significance. And they followed one another night after night in a bewildering procession.

He covered a few fires, one of which was a three-alarm spectacle in a granary on the river that merited a top head on the first page. He developed a knack for writing short human interest features and so became acquainted with a weird galaxy of inventors with a variety of gadgets for extracting valuable products from garbage, sharpening razor blades, squaring the circle, or mobilizing the fish in Lake Michigan. One of these geniuses had perfected a new spring suspension for horse-drawn buggies, and another hoped to make his fortune with a process for aging whisky in twenty minutes. He wrote of them sadly and with much forbearance because there weren't any buggies in town anymore and the current crop of bootleggers' customers didn't seem to care much whether whisky was aged or not.

In other phases of his research into the accomplishments and afflictions of Chicago's little people he interviewed dozens of little girls who had lost their dogs. He wrote of old circus clowns, soap sculptors, and wandering children. He covered neighborhood art exhibits and boys' club band concerts and orphans' picnics. And he found that in the main the people of the metropolis were much the same as those he had known in Ligonier.

The newspaper veterans who were bearing the heat and burden of the day when he came to the *Examiner* as a shy cub remember him in the last days of his journalistic career as a lad of much promise whose competence was considerably greater than his experience. He lacked the zany characteristics so prevalent among the shock troops of the staff. He had none of the swaggering impudence that was supposed to be an essential in a reporter's attitude toward his public. But he had other qualifications that would have made him great had he chosen to stay in the newspaper business. "He never seemed to meet any strangers," the late Frank Carson once said of him. "People liked him automatically and trusted him — and what's more, they talked to him."

His associates mention the short period when, like all reporters at one time or another, he took his turn covering the police beat. He didn't know much about police routine or the cutthroat policies of the boys in the pressroom. But it made no difference. "People liked him automatically" — and that included the cops. . . . . "And what's more they talked to him." He has friends high in the department to-day whom he met as patrolmen at Central station. It is significant that however brief their early acquaintance he can still call them all by name.

Dwight Green remained on the *Examiner's* staff until September, when he had to go back to his law classes at the University. Then despite Carson's pleading and promises, he left the newspaper business for good.

"You are throwing away a great opportunity," Carson told him. "And you won't like the law. There's no future in it. It's just about as interesting as running a steam laundry and it's more uncertain. It'll bore you stiff."

"Well, maybe," admitted young Mr. Green, and he felt at the moment as if he were looking both ways from the crossroads. He had a deep respect for Carson's judgment. But he went anyway. He had a lot of his grandfather's persistence. . . . . And as for uncertainty! Well his initiation into journalism was still too recent to be hazy in his memory.

— 10 —

THE HOODLUMS DIG IN

THERE WASN'T MUCH IN THE EXPERIENCE OF Dwight Green to discount Carson's prophecy during the next two years. In his last semester at the University he began to find in the law some of the interest he had expected of it — so much, in fact, that he gave up his job as campus correspondent for the *Examiner* to give his whole time to it. A principal factor in arousing this interest was Daddy Mechem, the great professor on partnership and agency, whose impact on the mind of Dwight Green in his law-school years was similar to that of Rollo Brown in his years at Wabash.

When he went onto campus, he found the law fraternity Phi Alpha Delta inactive. The young would-be lawyer set out to reorganize it. He did. Phi Alpha Delta at the University of Chicago became not only an active and going chapter, but through Dwight Green's efforts it got a fraternity house. Athletics was forsaken and what spare time he had was devoted to his fraternity. Phi Alpha Delta remembered this service when, in 1936, Dwight H. Green was elected Supreme Justice of the fraternity.

He experienced the usual thrill when he was graduated in June, 1922, and felt that life was beginning for him when he was admitted to the bar in the fall of the same year. He felt some satisfaction when he returned to Roy Keehn's office as a legal assistant instead of a clerk. But thereafter for many months he got his fill of routine work.

During 1923 John Torrio never became the target for any great hue and cry. He seems to have received sporadic publicity in the prohibition stories merely because other active bootleggers hadn't yet done anything to impair their anonymity. As Colosimo's ex-bodyguard and spiritual heir, Torrio was ticketed in the newspaper morgues as de facto overlord of the First Ward. The flow of homemade intoxicants through that ward was beginning to be noticeable, and by innuendo if not by any useless charges in court Torrio was sometimes suggested as the responsible source of it. Dion O'Banion, the onetime safeblower unofficially credited with having been a truckmaster for Torrio, was named once or twice as the organizer of an independent beer and liquor supply business on the north side. "Scarface" Al Brown Capone wasn't mentioned in the public prints at all.

Out of his own experience and through frequent meetings with his old city-room associates the young man from Ligonier was able to provide himself with plenty of unprintable facts to augment what he read in the daily press. Despite the fact that most of the people of Chicago continued to see, speak, and hear no evil, he strung together

enough isolated facts and rumors and shrewd guesses
to convince himself that the illegal alcohol business was
expanding at an incredible and appalling rate. Even considering its staggering operating cost in graft, its net income promised to make it the nation's greatest and most
profitable enterprise. It was preposterous to suppose that
with millions of dollars at stake any one man or single
group could hope to maintain a monopoly in it even in
one city the size of Chicago. The usefulness of the so-
called gentlemen's agreements that had so far governed
the local trade seemed just about finished. So he was one
member of the community who was not surprised when
the city was shaken out of its complacency by the opening
blasts of the gang war in the fall of 1923.

As the result of investigations brought about by murders
that even an apathetic chief of police was compelled to
recognize as such, the public became aware of some of
the facts that had been set down in Green's dossier months
before. Beer had become the most important item in the
bootlegger's catalogue, and the difficulty of distributing it
— a consideration that during 1920 and 1921 had immersed
the municipalities of the United States in bathtub gin —
had been removed by efficient organization and official
connivance. John Torrio had taken over the big West
Hammond brewery. He had acquired a fine fleet of modern
trucks, doubled his mob of thugs, and worked out a
delivery system that would have been the envy of any
great legitimate mercantile establishment. He had planned
to serve retailers — whether they liked it or not — anywhere inside the city limits. But he hadn't worked fast

enough. His former lieutenant, O'Banion, had found a
source of supply on the North Side. And in the stockyards district — which he looked upon as his own back
yard — he suddenly came upon serious competition from a
picturesque family — Steve, Walter, Thomas, and "Spike"
O'Donnell — later identified in print as "the South Side
O'Donnells" to distinguish them from "the West Side
O'Donnells" (Myles and Klondike) who were in the same
sort of business but not related.

For the first two years of prohibition the South Side
O'Donnells had been running a brewery in a small way
but, thanks to Torrio's political connections, hadn't given
him serious competition. In 1923, however, there was a
change in the city administration, with inevitable effects
on the status quo of the protection system. The four
brothers were quick to see their opportunity. The market
was wide open, and their beer was better than Torrio's.
The connoisseurs of the stockyards and adjoining districts
gave them ready custom.

Torrio who was a businessman first and a gangster second — so long as there was any possible profit in that
arrangement — met the competition in a businesslike manner. He cut the price of his beer ten dollars a barrel. The
O'Donnells lacked his organization and financial resources,
but they had inventiveness and a realistic attitude toward
their trade. Why bother with operating agreements and
price lists and such things as supply and demand in what
was essentially a racket? In keeping with this practical
philosophy, they devised and put into effect the system
of terrorizing speakeasy operators who tried to sell any

other beer but theirs. A less perspicacious observer than Dwight Green might easily have figured where such a course was going to lead.

On September 7, 1923, Jerry O'Connor, a young hoodlum acting as agent for the O'Donnells, went out with three of the brothers — Steve, Walter and Tommy — to impress the merits of their product on a few recalcitrants. The quartet came in due course to the saloon operated by one John Kepka at 5358 South Lincoln Street. There they learned for the first time that John Torrio had lost faith in the effectiveness of price cutting. Kepka was not alone in his speakeasy. Four Torrio mobsters were standing at the bar when the O'Donnell sales party came in.

Somebody turned out the lights and the shooting started without further preliminary. When the police arrived ten minutes later, O'Connor lay dead on the floor, and they found Kepka cowering behind the bar. But they got no information about what had happened. It was dark, said Kepka. And besides he was lying flat on his face trying to keep out of the way of the bullets.

Later that night the police picked up a brace of hoodlums, who were turned loose before their lawyers could start habeas corpus proceedings because the chief of police "had no reason" for holding them. And that ended the first killing of a series that was to run up into the hundreds.

Ten days later there were two more murders. George Meegan and George Bucher were shot, presumably because they had threatened to tell who killed O'Connor. State's Attorney Robert E. Crowe announced that he was beginning a "relentless investigation" of the beer war.

Orders were issued for the arrest of John Torrio, but before a squad could get over to his office he appeared in the state's attorney's office with his attorney. It is characteristic of Torrio's methods that he seldom waited to be arrested.

Nothing happened to him, of course, save that he got a lot of publicity that he may not have wanted. He emerged from his conference with Mr. Crowe with the reputation of being the directing intelligence of the biggest beer-running syndicate in the United States.

In December, 1923, Morrie Keane and William Egan, minor factors in Torrio's competition, started for Chicago one night from Joliet as a convoy to three truckloads of beer. About halfway to Chicago they were halted by a crew of Torrio hijackers under the direction of Frank Mc Erlane, a gunman with a record antedating prohibition. They were forced into McErlane's car and taken away. They were found, shot to death, by the roadside the next morning.

A truck driver who escaped this shambles turned up to testify against McErlane, who was arrested, held by the state's attorney for a time in a loop hotel, and released. After an indignant uproar in the newspapers, he was indicted. But months afterward the case against him was nolle prossed, and Mr. McErlane lived to take an active part in neighborhood politics.

That ended the murder record for 1923. In view of the statistics that the gangs wrote into the mortuary reports in later years, it doesn't seem to have been any more important than Chicago's public officials considered it. But the lull in the gin and beer business was definitely ended. Torrio's privacy had been destroyed for good. Federal investigation of the West Hammond Brewery, now known as the Puro Products Co., had indicated that he was operating with a payroll of $25,000 a week — which adds up to $1,300,000 a year. No Chicagoan in his right mind believed that the activities of an institution with enough cash balance to permit that kind of overhead were going to stop at half a dozen killings. And they didn't.

In April, 1924, displaying a technique later favored by Adolph Hitler, Torrio moved in force into Cicero, an undistinguished but peaceful suburb adjoining Chicago's West Side. The maneuver at the time was not properly appraised, nor did its aims and ramifications become evident until prohibition had nearly run its course. But it might have been recognized by any student of current events as an indication of the lengths to which Torrio intended to expand.

With the change of administration in 1923, he was harried by that familiar bugaboo of big business, increasing cost of operation. He still had plenty of friends in the First Ward, and his influence was being felt in the courts. But he had built up an organization designed to care for the needs of the whole city, if not the whole of Cook County, and it seemed bad strategy to maintain headquarters in a community that was only partly friendly.

Furthermore, he had that foresight of an ice-box manufacturer who tools up to produce hats and radio tubes and widgets as a hedge against a possible decrease in the demand for his principal line. The established brothels of the old levee were still delivering important revenues, but he didn't expect them to survive the reform wave. Gambling, long in control of a tight little group of old established specialists, had become another of Chicago's uncertainties. And there was plenty of money to be made in gambling if one could find a place for it where the authorities could be made to listen to reason.

The suburbs appealed to him. The county officials didn't seem to be sharing any of the city's unpredictable trends toward prudery, and it is an elementary principle of strategy that you don't need as much force to take over a small town as you do to hold onto a big one. He opened up several gambling houses in Burnham and Stickney, and the results were up to his expectations. Then, in the fall of 1923, he began a campaign of infiltration as a preliminary to the capture of Cicero. He opened a brothel on Roosevelt Road.

He had had no trouble in Burnham or Stickney — at least his invasion of those towns had made no work for the coroner. But in Cicero he encountered opposition. Eddie Tancl, former prizefighter and popular hero among the Bohemian population, was running a prosperous cafe in Cicero, and he saw no good in Torrio.

Soon after it opened, Torrio's place was wrecked by the Cicero police. He moved the personnel over to a building on Ogden Avenue, and the Cicero police wrecked it again. Sheriff Peter Hoffman then sent a squad of deputies into the town to raid the slot machines operated by Torrio's antagonists, who capitulated at once. There were no palavers or formal agreements, but a week later the slot machines came back, and Torrio reopened his brothel without molestation.

He branched out a little during the remaining weeks of 1923. He opened a gambling house that was immediately successful. But he was still moving cautiously in a sort of armed truce. Tancl was still strong in popular favor. Some local factions were still anything but cordial, and so far as his freedom of action was concerned he was little better off here than inside the city limits. However, nobody ever condemned John Torrio for his lack of patience. If he waited long enough, he felt, he could provide the continuance of a friendly administration and get complete control of the town. While marking time he found it profitable to show little kindnesses to public officials and key citizens — he arranged for the repair (gratis) of the homes of his new-found friends, paid off a few mortgages, gained the esteem of housewives (suitably connected) with gifts of ice boxes and washing machines, and spread a considerable largess of cash where it would do the most good. And he didn't have to wait long for results — only until April 1, 1924, election day.

In one way and another, save for the uncertainty surrounding his experiments in gambling and prostitution, he hadn't done too badly in the interim. More than a hundred saloons were selling his beer, and, it is said, quite a few office-holders had accepted nominal positions on the payroll of his syndicate and, in private at least, looked upon him as a worthy addition to the community. The difficulty was that, publicly, these official friends had to maintain an air of neutrality amid the outcries of Tancl's followers and other groups threatening reprisals in behalf of good citizenship. Politically, they were in no little danger of being voted out of their jobs — in which event they would be of no use to Torrio whatever. So Torrio took steps to insure their permanence.

The 1924 election in Cicero was another gang phenomenon of the sort identified with the rise of Hitler. Certainly it was a spectacle of a sort seldom, if ever, beheld in an American city since the passing of the James brothers. Into the town on the morning of April 1, openly and in the spirit of gay carnival, roared Torrio's gestapo, a hundred or more strong.

There had been a few preliminaries. Election Commissioner Anthony Czarnecki had scratched 3,000 names of alleged voters, most of whom were at the moment residing in cemeteries, from the Cicero register. He had discharged large numbers of clerks, watchers, and judges and appointed others in their places. Torrio's rivals in the beer business, foreseeing a possible break in the local market monopoly, had lined up with money and physical support behind the opposition. On the eve of election gunmen had charged into the office of William K. Pflaum, antiadministration candidate for clerk, assaulted him with blackjacks, shot out the lights, and wrecked the premises. So nothing that happened after that came as much of a surprise.

The gunmen, none of them residents of Cicero, some of them not even citizens of the United States, opened their program under the leadership of Al Capone with a routine canvass of the polling places where, without protest from the cowed election officials, they voted at least once apiece for the friends of their chief. In front of the polls they parked cars with machine guns sticking through the windows. With pistols in their hands they sat among the clerks and briefly but definitely instructed prospective voters on how to cast their ballots. They set up deadlines a city block away from the voting booths, beyond which nobody who admitted a preference for an opposition candidate was allowed to step.

They were full of confidence and boyish horseplay and at first tried to maintain the quarantine without too much bloodshed. As a preliminary warning they shot their pistols into the air, and the only danger to the citizenry lay in the fact that bullets which go up must also come down. But the boys were firm when they had to be. If any member of Cicero's free electorate made the mistake of arguing with them, they shot him.

All morning the town echoed to gunfire like a preview of Iwo Jima. A good half of the population went home and locked the doors. If the local police put in any appearance at all, they watched the prankish performance of the visiting gunmen as one might look at a Fourth of July celebration and dismissed the complaints of the proletariat as unwarranted hysteria.

Says the Chicago Crime Commission's report: "Automobiles filled with gunmen paraded the streets, slugging and kidnaping election workers. Polling places were raided by armed thugs and ballots were taken at the point of the gun from voters waiting to drop them into a box. Voters and workers were kidnaped, brought to Chicago, and held prisoners until the polls closed. Stanley Stanklevich, a worker, was among the first kidnaped. He was held prisoner in a basement until 8 o'clock. Michael Gavin was kidnaped and found shot through both legs; he was imprisoned with eight others. . . . ."

The Hoodlums Dig In

All morning long the telephones were ringing in the County Building in Chicago. Jittery messengers came in relays to the offices of Sheriff Hoffman and County Judge Jarecki. One unidentified citizen got in touch with the Governor in Springfield and demanded that he call out the troops. And as a result of all this Judge Jarecki deputized seventy patrolmen, five squads from the detective bureau, and nine flivver squads and rushed them to Cicero.

This mobilization was one of the biggest the Chicago district had seen since the Haymarket riots, but it is still a matter of local belief that the police were outnumbered by the hoodlums, whose forces had been increasing steadily since daybreak. This is purely a matter of academic interest, for if there was any discrepancy in numbers it doesn't seem to have bothered the police very much. They succeeded in chasing literally scores of Torrio-Capone gunmen out of town.

The maneuvering was punctuated with sporadic battles that speedily began to fill up the hospitals. But the climax of the day came when, as Detective Sergeant William Cusack and his squad were passing a polling place, three men rushed out and opened fire on them with pistols. The police answered with pistols and shotguns, and some fifty shots were exchanged in a battle from which all the gaiety of the morning had departed. Two hoodlums presently fell, one of them stone cold dead on the sidewalk, the other bleeding from half a dozen wounds.

Some semblance of order came back to the town after that. The gangsters had gone into hiding or back to Chicago. All the saloons were untenanted and locked, their curtains drawn. Anti-administration watchers came back to the polls.

But none of these things had any appreciable effect on the results. When the ballots were counted, Torrio's friends were back in office. Four men were dead .... forty wounded.

It was some time before Cusack and his squad were able to identify the man they had sent to the morgue. And when they did, it seemed a matter of no consequence. He was a lad who had been associated with Torrio from the beginning — a sort of run-of-the-mill gangster who had done his work without attracting public attention — and never before had engaged in open gunplay with the law.

His name was Frank Capone. The police remembered after a while that he had a brother with a scarred face, a minor tough sometimes known as Al Brown who was a roustabout or something in the Four Deuces dive on Wabash Avenue.

Frank got a fine funeral. He was laid away in a silver-plated coffin, and his tastefully selected grave was strewn with $20,000 worth of lilies and wreaths bearing such legends as "We mourn our loss," "Gone but not forgotten," and similar poesy.

The flowers, for the most part, came from the shop of Dion O'Banion, the former Torrio truck driver who had set himself up in a little independent business on the North Side to deal in bouquets and beer — but mostly beer.

11

THE START OF A NEW TECHNIQUE

THE KILLING OF FRANK CAPONE, WHICH WAS generally looked upon as an inconsequential incident in a public outrage, caused no stir in Chicago. The newspapers weren't much interested in his biography. The only result of his passing that seems worth mentioning is the fact that it brought the name of his brother Alphonse into the public prints for the first time. And nobody paid any attention to that.

The capture of Cicero was another matter. There were still plenty of people in the community who remembered what they had been told about the sovereign rights of the citizen in a democracy, the power of the ballot, the sanctity of free elections — and public indignation and protest went on endlessly. Civic associations demanded action that they didn't get. The county authorities advertised investigations which produced nothing save some evidence that hoodlums had been active at the polls. There was some wild talk about Federal intervention. But the tally was in — and so was Torrio. Nothing, apparently, could be done about it.

For the first time in his life young Dwight Green began to have his doubts about the majesty of the law. All of this gang activity meant nothing to him, of course, save what it must mean to any citizen of a civilized state. Something must be wrong with a system that permitted mob control of an election and admitted its own helplessness in dealing with the result. What was the use of Magna Cartas and Bills of Rights and Constitutions that could be emasculated by official greed? What price all these libraries of learned decisions that presumably defined the rights of the people in a free country? What, after all, was the sense of talking about democracy in a nation where insolent criminals had the final word in the molding of government? What was the purpose of grinding one's brains to prepare cases for courts whose decisions were dictated from the back rooms of saloons and the parlors of brothels? A fledgling lawyer certainly could be excused such questions, and just as certainly he could not be expected to know the answers.

The isolated case of an election in a small municipality, he felt, might be insignificant in the affairs of a hundred million people. But the conditions that had brought it about could not conceivably be looked upon as something of peculiarly local concern. He needed no second sight to realize that what had happened in one town could happen in another. Whatever the benign purpose of the prohibition amendment it was affording the lawbreakers a war chest without equal in the history of sin. There was no limit to what men like Torrio could do with pocketfuls of thousand-dollar bills. Neither, he found every reason to believe, was there any limit to their ambitions. The gangsters weren't going to be content with a successful campaign in Cicero.

It came to him forcibly that perhaps Carson had been right, that the law offered no future. There was increasing evidence that it had no future — that as a science it was as obsolete as fortune telling. His doubts lingered for a long time.

Roy Keehn, to whom he took his troubles, gave him some encouragement.

"There aren't any perfect institutions on this earth," he said. "Civilization is a cumbersome affair, and democratic government is one of its least finished products. The machinery just isn't self-adjusting — not yet. A large percentage of the legislation on our books has been enacted to correct the defects of other legislation, and we're a long way from any simple formula to deal with human relationships. But you've got to take the long view of it. Here and there a few public servants get tired of being honest, and justice goes out the window. Sometimes the thug element manages to throttle a government and you have despotisms and dictatorships. But the point is that they don't last. In the long run the law always wins. . . . ."

Dwight Green managed to keep this in his mind during the grim years that followed; instinctively he realized its truth, although at times his faith was severely tested. As he had foreseen, the gangs were to go a long way before their dissolution.

As time went on the name of Al Capone seemed to be

constantly in his ears. The details escaped him, but vaguely he remembered having had some fleeting contact with this unpleasant character in his days on the *Examiner*. So it piqued his interest when Al was mentioned in the accounts of the inquest into the death of his brother Frank. There was nothing enlightening in the newspaper paragraph — nothing to indicate why his name in print should have brought to Green's mind the nebulous picture of a cross-hatched, sweaty face with cold eyes and a sneering mouth. Al, an eye witness to the battle with the police, had been summoned to testify and had said only that he had nothing to say.

On May 8, 1924, the recluse of the Four Deuces got into the papers again. He was being "sought for questioning," as journalistic double talk put it, in connection with the casual murder of one Joseph Howard.

There never was a more public or better authenticated murder in Chicago than the taking off of Mr. Howard. He had entered the Four Deuces and had sat down at a table as a customer. He was sitting down, apparently oblivious of danger, when Al Brown-Capone came in and, without warning or other preliminaries, shot him dead.

Probably a dozen employees and customers of the dive saw the murder in all its details, and they weren't ordinary witnesses. As habitues of the place they all knew Capone. Most of them were acquainted with the victim. And they were a voluble lot.

Before morning the minutes of the meeting had been spread from one end of Chicago to the other. There was some disagreement concerning the motive for the killing. Howard had been unkind to a Four Deuces waiter favored by Brown — a waiter named Jake Guzik. . . . . Howard had failed to show proper grief over the death of Frank Capone. . . . . Howard had been volubly critical of Al Brown's prowess and methods. . . . . Anybody's theory was as good as anybody else's. But there was never any doubt about what had happened and who did it. One unacquainted with the processes of gangdom might logically have prophesied Al's early death on the gallows.

But there were reasons why such a happy ending to the story of Joseph Howard would never be written. The witnesses who were able and willing to talk like rag merchants among their own kind proved shy and embarrassed when it came to conversation with visiting detectives. All that the police were able to establish officially was that somebody nobody had ever seen before walked into the Four Deuces and had shot the man nobody knew. Even the Four Deuces might have remained anonymous save for the fact that a corpse had been found on the barroom floor.

The search for Capone — such as it was — went on for more than a month without result. By that time the fugitive had completed his estimate of the situation and gave himself up. On June 11, he surrendered at the Cottage Grove Avenue Station to Assistant State's Attorney William Mc-Swiggin. That, two years later, he was to be mentioned in connection with McSwiggin's murder is another of those coincidental dramatic touches that seem so striking in retrospect.

Capone, whose painless notoriety had assured him place among the more newsworthy characters of the gang narratives, was released without undue delay, and after that he

12

CAPONE TAKES OVER

ORRIO WAS GRANTED AN APPEAL, POSTED BOND, and prepared to take up his work where the Sieben brewery raid had interrupted it. He assigned Al Capone to extend his gambling operations in Cicero — an undertaking that was expedited by the killing of Eddie Tancl. And once more he made widespread pleas for more gentlemanly conduct in the trade. But he never again got such tangible assurances of co-operation as those that resulted in his arrest. The signs on his horizon were still too dim to be noticeable, but John Torrio was on his way out the day he heard his sentence.

Dion O'Banion, still to be tried, was stirring up trouble at a time when Torrio didn't want any. Dion O'Banion had been running an independent business for a long time; despite his observance of certain amenities in competition with his former mentor, he was a difficult man to argue with. As a matter of pretty sentiment he had bought a partnership in a florist's shop opposite Holy Name Cathedral where, as a boy, he had sung in the choir. In a less sentimental role he sold alcohol at $5 a gallon. And while Torrio was trying to keep himself out of jail, O'Banion had become annoyed with the Genna brothers, a West Side family, who were peddling a species of recooked canned heat for $2 a gallon.

O'Banion, who had none of Torrio's sense of the proprieties and stood in high regard among his associates as a killer, served the customary cease-and-desist notice on the Gennas, who refused to pay any attention to him. Instead, they went out to Cicero to petition the aid of Al Capone.

The Gennas had grown prosperous in association with John Torrio and had never had an open break with him, even when they set up a business of their own in "Little Sicily." On the other hand they hadn't been contributing much to his organization. They had taken alcohol production off the assembly line and put it back in the hands of individual craftsmen who lived on the West Side and tended little stills in their basements. They distributed it wherever they found a market at $2 a gallon, and so far had had little need for any over-large troop of hoodlums.

Torrio, still hopeful of getting the numerous factions of the industry to reach some sort of working agreement, might not have been willing to lend a hand in a battle with O'Banion. Capone, now grown great and in full command of Torrio's Cicero garrison, turned a more receptive ear. So far as he was concerned, the Gennas didn't amount to anything. But they were old acquaintances. They were giving a lot of trouble to the West Side O'Donnells (Klon-

young opportunist, Al Capone. But so far as Torrio was concerned it was an academic discussion. Whoever was responsible, he felt that the situation had got well out of hand. When, with time off for good behavior, he completed his sentence six weeks before the end of the specified nine months, three carloads of trusted lads from the old brigade were waiting for him at the door of the jail. They drove him to Buffalo, went on by train with him to New York, and saw him off on a ship to Italy.

At home, Al Capone was already well established in the leadership of the abandoned syndicate. And whether Capone had come into this legacy through friendship or the application of a little judicious terrorism, he had no time to think about the plight of his onetime benefactor. He had trouble of his own — plenty of trouble. He was involved in the most hideous campaign of murder ever seen on American soil.

To give him what little credit may be his due, he was not entirely to blame for the unprecedented boom in Cook County's undertaking business. He gave a corporationlike efficiency to the business, developed new techniques, and eventually hit upon a remarkably successful device known in other climes as the mass purge. Not until the Capone method was adopted by Hitler and Stalin did anybody, anywhere, surpass the St. Valentine's Day massacre. But for all his skill in slaughter, wholesale and retail, he might have been willing to consider an armistice after the dazzling obsequies of O'Banion had it not been for the fanatically vengeful dispositions of the North Side mob's new leaders.

Louie Alterie, who had offered to shoot it out with the

murderer of O'Banion at State and Madison streets, had been eased out of town by his own friends, not because of his intentions but because of his lack of finesse. Hymie Weiss, O'Banion's successor, is generally believed to have been only half-sane in his lucid moments; he was never any less blatant or more cautious than Alterie. But he had learned that in murder, as in every other pursuit, success comes most often to the craftsman who does a little preliminary spadework.

Weiss had been the one-man dog of his late chief, and he became a killer with a mission. His simple idea seems to have been that, since it was difficult to determine the identity of the man who had shot O'Banion, it would be necessary to make sure of him by slaughtering everybody in the old Torrio organization, including Al Capone.

Even before the attack on Torrio, North Side gangsters had blasted Capone's car and wounded Sylvester Barton, his chauffeur. Capone, by some odd break of luck, had come out unscathed. Temporarily Weiss turned his attention toward the immediate cause of O'Banion's final difficulties — the Genna brothers.

On May 26, 1925, Angelo Genna, reputed to be the toughest member of the wild little group, was filled with slugs by some gangster who had caught up with his car. This was the first fatality in a family that had taken part in an estimated dozen murders. The grief-stricken survivors were outraged. Over Angelo's badly damaged body they swore vengeance with the picturesque old Sicilian ceremony of crossed knives. To assist them in the discharge of their vows they enlisted John Scalise and Albert Anselmi, a pair of bravos with prison records in the old country,

see again, such unreasoning hate. After the failure of one of their efforts to remove Capone, the leaders of the vendetta captured his chauffeur, whom they tortured literally for hours in an attempt to get some information about his future movements. When at the end of his ordeal the chauffeur refused to tell them what they wanted to know, they shot him and dumped his body into a well in East Chicago.

In mounting rage they abandoned even ordinary gang precautions and one bright day moved boldly, three carloads of them, into Cicero. Capone's mobsters had been warned in advance of their coming and by the time Weiss led his caravan on the slow canvass of the town, all the local gunmen were in hiding. The North Siders, after vain efforts to provoke a battle, took a leisurely and unmolested course to the Hawthorne Smoke Shop, Capone's post of command. And while the inmates — including Capone — cowered behind steel shutters, they shattered the front of the building with the concentrated fire of three or four machine guns, wounding four people. But the police made no attempt to stop the mobsters as they left town.

The South Siders made an attempt at retaliation a week later by ramming Weiss's car at high noon in Michigan Avenue and taking potshots at him and "Schemer" Drucci, who was riding with him. Weiss and Drucci managed to run into the Standard Oil Building, unharmed. And shortly after that Capone sent word that he was willing to agree to an armistice.

Weiss was too busy nursing his hate to want peace. He sent back a reply that he would discuss the matter only when Capone had agreed to "put on the spot" (i.e., stake out for slaughter) the two men who had taken part in the Michigan Avenue ambush. Capone reluctantly refused, and the terrorism went on to new climaxes. The death roll became so long that even the coroner could no longer recount the names of the victims offhand: Walter O'Donnell, George "Big Bates" Karl, William Dickman, Charles Kelly, Ed Lattyak, Pasquale Tolizotte, "Dynamite Joe" Brooks, County Policeman Edward Harmening, Frank De-Laurentis, John Tucello, Frank Conlon, John "Mitters" Foley, Tony Campagna, Sam Lavenuto, James Russo, Henry Spignola (brother-in-law of the Gennas), Augustino Moreci, Antonio Moreci, Orazio Tropea, Vito Bascone, Eddie Baldelli, Tony Finalli, Samuzzo Amatuna. . . .

Some of these murders were incident to the rise of the Joe Saltis-Frank McErlane hijacking and beer-running combination, which prospered while Capone was occupied with the North Side mob. Others grew out of jurisdictional disputes that naturally followed the elimination of the Gennas from the home-cooked alcohol industry. Not a few resulted from the methods of thugs sent out to raise a $100,-000 defense fund for Scalise and Anselmi. But fundamentally they were all part of the same picture. Generically as well as chronologically they all stemmed from Capone's determination to maintain an undisputed control over Chicago.

The issue was still in doubt when the young man who was one day to destroy Capone left Chicago for Washington in the fall of 1925. But he never lacked for news of the bloody progress of the struggle. The newspapers of the world were filled with it.

tradition in the matter of Senate rules, the sale of the Dodge Brothers Automobile Company for $146,000,000, the biggest cash transaction in American history and a startling indication of how far the motor industry had come in a single decade, the rise of the dollar in world markets, the indignation of Japan over restrictions on immigration, the operation of the Dawes Plan in Germany, the beginning of such income tax payments as John D. Rockefeller Jr.'s $7,435,-169. Taking the broad view of it, the United States of America was going along much as usual in spite of the Roman holiday in Chicago.

In the fall of 1925, just when the local gang war was well along toward a peak production of a corpse a day, Dwight Green received a favorable reply to an application for a place on the legal staff of the Bureau of Internal Revenue. It would be pleasant to say that at this turning point in his life he had been granted a vision — that he saw, even dimly, an opportunity to end the greatest scourge ever visited upon a civilized community. But, as a matter of fact, he did what he did from entirely practical purposes. He had no more daydreams than any other smart young hardheaded realist. He had no premonitions other than the conviction that he would one day make a success in his profession. And if he went out from Keehn's office a potential knight in shining armor, he was the last person in the place to know about it.

"Three or four friends who were in law school with me were working as special attorneys in the Bureau of Internal Revenue," is the way he recalls it. "They kept writing to me that it was the sort of work I'd like and that they could get me placed in the office of the general counsel. So I made the application and I went to Washington."

As a special attorney in the Revenue Bureau, he found living considerably more pleasant than it had been in Chicago. For the first time in his life he got a salary big enough to obviate the necessity for skimping on meals and lodging. And the work, although he had had no special training for it, came easy to him. Figures were figures, and basic law was basic law, and the tax problems that came to his attention in Washington weren't much different from those he'd heard about in the bank in Ligonier except that the totals were bigger.

He was first assigned to Interpretive Division I, the opening gambit for all newcomers to the Bureau's legal department. There for nine months he wrote opinions on questions involving an interpretation of the revenue laws. After that he was transferred to the Board of Tax Appeals Division where, until 1927, he got plenty of practice trying cases before the Board.

His appointment to Washington was a good thing for him, even had it not led to fame and a governorship — if only because it completely restored his faith in the power and permanence of government. The efficient administration of the income tax law and the high level of honesty surrounding it amazed him. For once he was permitted a slight glimpse at the future, and he foresaw a time when the enforced accounting for all receipts and expenditures by corporations as well as individuals would eliminate the "black bags" that had controlled the vote of legislatures. His theorizing took no particular direction or form, but

ch., stores, schl., transp., rsnble." She is more interested in politics now than she was before her marriage, but perhaps she may be excused for that.

Dwight Green brought his wife back with him to Chicago in February, 1927. He was thirty years old and beginning to make a name for himself as one of the smartest tax experts in the Bureau. His assignment to the Federal District of Northern Illinois was important, surprisingly important for a man of his years. But it came to him on the strength of his performance in the division of tax appeals. He had no political connections or friends at court.

His official title was "special assistant to the general counsel of the U. S. Bureau of Internal Revenue." In practice he was adviser and attorney for the local collector of internal revenue, revenue agents, special agents, and agents of the special intelligence division of the Treasury Department.

In addition to that he was presently given an appointment as assistant U. S. district attorney. For a young man who had never sought honors, he was collecting gold braid at an unprecedented rate.

On his arrival from Washington he conferred with George E. Q. Johnson who had been named U. S. district attorney three weeks before. Johnson's docket was filled with income tax cases, and he welcomed the assistance of the new special attorney as a gift from heaven.

"I'll give you all of these cases to handle," he said, "and I'll arrange to get you what help you need."

One thing led to another. Johnson found quarters for him in the Federal Building close to his own. When Green's preparation of cases was completed, he had to be qualified to appear before the Federal grand jury. This, as a matter of routine, resulted in his appointment as special assistant U. S. attorney. In due course and for the same reason he was named special assistant attorney general. The titles were important legally but otherwise unprofitable. He got no pay from the Department of Justice which conferred them. Always his pay check came to him from the Treasury Department, and it was some time before it got any larger.

14

"FIRST CATCH YOUR GANGSTER"

Dwight Green's plan for striking at the gangsters through the revenue law was less nebulous when he came back to Chicago than it had been during his early days in Washington. But it was still a long way from practical form. . . . . "First catch your gangster!". . . . . And the gangsters with all the money necessary to buy the best legal talent in the world were well advised and wary.

He takes no credit for sole authorship of the idea.

"There were lots of different agents working on these cases," he says, "and many of them kept books on the so-called 'big shots' in the mobs. They made a practice of clipping newspaper paragraphs about these people on occasions when they made a display of money. Here'd be something about one individual who had lost a lot of money at the race track. Well, the question was, where did he get the money before he lost it and how much was it?

"So that went into the file along with stories of how Capone gave away diamond belt buckles and how some other hoodlum like "Smoots" Amatuna had a couple of hundred silk shirts and how the boys in the North Side mob owned two or three automobiles apiece — without visible means of support. The gangsters never publicly spent a dime that wasn't duly recorded in their dossiers. And the accumulative effect of these sporadic and seemingly futile jottings was enormous in later trials."

There is no doubt, however, that the finished technique by which the tax law was finally brought to bear against the gangs was Green's. He worked over it for nearly a year before he felt safe in trying it out in a court. It is one thing to argue a technical point of law with lawyers — quite another to bring the same point home to a jury of laymen — and the use of the revenue act for the purpose of stopping a murder epidemic was nothing if not technical.

In his work as legal adviser to the Federal investigators he got a chance to study all the phases of tax evasion. At all times he worked with the collector, the revenue agents, and the special agents whose functions are definite and distinct. The revenue agents, for example are charged with the handling of civil cases involving honest miscalculation and underpayment of tax. They make an investigation and turn in a report. On the basis of their reports demand for additional taxes may be made. Where fraud is indicated they turn the case over to agents of the special intelligence unit of the Treasury Department, whose duty it is to investigate and prepare criminal cases, and in all of these inquiries the legal adviser has a prominent and continuous part.

"I worked with the agents in questioning witnesses or in discussions of the procedure to be followed in getting certain evidence." Green recalls. "The examination of bank accounts, for instance, is a ticklish and technical job, and it had to be done properly. You had, at least, to lay the proper groundwork so that when an agent went to a bank — or anywhere else, as far as that's concerned — to get information, he wouldn't be running into legal technicalities and making mistakes that might mix up the whole procedure."

He had known a lot about that sort of work before leaving Washington. He knew most of the time-honored methods for concealing assets and quite a few new ones. But he was to learn a lot more in the unencouraging labor of 1927. He found out among other things that the gangsters were one group of idle rich who feared the banks. Like misers, they hoarded their money in boxes where they could get at it. The only difference was that they hoarded more of it at a time.

Like Henry Ford in the days of his rise, the basis of their operations was strictly cash — a novelty that may have interested Green as an economist but discouraged him as an investigator. The files showed that Capone during the first year after the abdication of Torrio had been doing a business of $70,000,000. His annual turnover now might well be $100,000,000, but there seemed to be slight chance of proving it. Capone issued no annual statements to stockholders. He employed no auditors as yet discovered. His revenue appeared in no bank records, and certainly there was no trace of it in his income tax returns.

"First Catch Your Gangster"

Probably there will never again be a melodrama in Chicago with a climax like the smashing of Capone, but just as certainly there will never be one to approach it in the dullness of its first few acts. Raids on the Capone syndicate's enterprises in Cicero went on with endless monotony — the prohibition enforcement authorities were lending a hand willingly but ineffectively. Always the mobsters were warned in advance of the raids. It was obvious to Green that the young man from Brooklyn was extending his influence beyond the municipal courts and county offices. There was evidence now that he had spies in the Federal Building. The raids brought to Green's mill no grist that he couldn't have discovered for himself in the newspapers. So his days and more than a hundred long, sleepless nights were passed in futile mathematics and the purposeless analysis of trivia.

Looking back on it one realizes that this was war — war against a spreading dictatorship as insidious as the one that in a few years was to bring about the mobilization of 10,-000,000 American soldiers. In the result they finally achieved, the men of the Federal Building showed themselves to be as strategically competent as any successful army in the field. But never did an army fight with poorer weapons, so little glory, and so scant a hope for success.

Dwight Green's name appears some times in the newspaper clippings of the period. But generally he is quoted as an authority on some phase of the revenue act. Occasionally he is interviewed concerning the case of some tax dodger currently on trial. He is treated with the respect due him as an expert with unusual acumen and high pro-

Capone, the wizard administrator, the magnificent leader. But postmortem eulogy doesn't alter the fact that by 1927 he had become not only a public enemy but a public nuisance.

For more than two years since the murder of Dion O'Banion, the murder crew of Hymie Weiss had gone on with its relentless work. Capone's men were found dead on their own doorsteps and in alleys all over town. Capone fought back diligently and promiscuously; sometimes after the day's hunting odd specimens indeed turned up in the bag.

On April 27, 1926, William H. McSwiggin, an assistant to State's Attorney Robert Crowe, was shot dead in front of a Cicero saloon by machine gunners still unidentified. With him were James Doherty and Thomas Duffy, a brace of expendable young thugs whose position in the beer-running racket was never definitely established. One school of thought linked them with Myles and Klondike O'Donnell, the "West Side" O'Donnells. On the other hand Doherty had been the choice suspect in the murder of Eddie Tancl — foeman of the Torrio-Capone interests in Cicero. This killing, for which he was duly prosecuted by the same William McSwiggin beside whose body he lay when the coroner caught up with him, would seem to have linked him with the South Side mob popularly credited with responsibility for McSwiggin's death. It all seemed too complicated for analysis at the time and still does.

There was an unusually loud popular outcry over the triple murder. Nobody cared much about Doherty and Duffy. Their going was hardly noticed by the beer-distributing industry and was regarded as a minor loss to the social life of Chicago. McSwiggin was a bright and pleasant youth with a gift for making friends. But had he had no friends at all, it would still have seemed a stupid idea to murder him, because his death provoked numerous charges of a connection between Chicago's law enforcement agencies and crime.

State's Attorney Crowe declared that his young assistant was a martyr to duty; that he had been associating with Doherty and Duffy to get information in an important murder case then pending; that it was possible he had been killed in revenge for his vigorous prosecution of Scalise and Anselmi, the law-proof assassins of the Genna gang.

Mayor Joseph Z. Klenha of Cicero said that the slaughter was a social error — that the machine gunners had mistaken McSwiggin and his companions for some of the O'Donnells. For reasons of their own the newspapers generally agreed with Police Sergeant Anthony McSwiggin, father of the murdered assistant state's attorney, that Al Capone and some of his aides had done the actual shooting. The *Chicago Examiner* continued for several weeks to ask the question in eight columns of black type across the top of the editorial page: "Who Killed McSwiggin and Why?" But ninety percent of Chicago's resentful citizens thought that they already knew the answers.

Capone made a characteristic observation on the unofficial suggestion that he might have had something to do with the murder. "I paid McSwiggin, and I paid him plenty," he stated. "I got what I was paying for, and I never had any reason to kill him." The "Big Fellow," it appears, was developing some sense of perspective. The payment of graft to politicians was just a sort of business

men came to watch these trips carefully as a sort of barometer of trouble — which, of course, they were.

He wasn't in town on October 11, 1926. He recalled afterward the exciting details of some dog races which, in company with a boxful of assorted hoodlums, he had watched that fateful afternoon. The hounds were running beautifully. The birds were twittering in the palm trees. And violence naturally was as far removed from his thoughts as it was from the scenes of pastoral loveliness about him. He was fortunate. In Chicago a lot of people would presently have been plaguing him with pointless but time-consuming questions.

With Capone out of town Hymie Weiss had been finding opportunity to busy himself with concerns aside from his vendetta. For a few days before October 11 he had been associating in an advisory capacity with the defense of Joe Saltis on trial for the murder of the late "Mitters" Foley. He had taken an active part in a social study of the veniremen who might possibly be chosen as jurors in the case; as a result of this no doubt useful work he had arranged for a conference with W. W. O'Brien, attorney for Saltis. At the Criminal Court Building he picked up O'Brien and Benjamin Jacobs, one of the lawyer's investigators. With this pair and Sam Peller, his chauffeur, and Patrick Murray, his bodyguard, he drove out to Dion O'Banion's old headquarters, the flower shop opposite Holy Name Cathedral. Peller found a parking space almost in front of the church door, and the party alighted to walk across the street.

As they came to the corner with Weiss and O'Brien in the lead, a machine-gun barrage spattered down on them from the bay window of a second-story flat at 740 North State Street, the building adjoining the flower shop. Twelve slugs hit Weiss and finished his campaign of vengeance some fifty feet from where it had started with the murder of O'Banion. Murray fell behind him dying. Peller and Jacobs were slightly wounded. O'Brien was in a hospital for months. The gunmen who had lain in ambush for ten days left the flat by the back stairs and succeeded in getting away.

The echoes of this impertinence were still reverberating when Dwight Green came back from Washington to open up the Capone file in the Federal Building. Among the worthy citizens who had been looking at the bloody activities of the gangsters with the fine detachment of spectators at a Punch and Judy show there was a growing sense of uneasiness approaching fear. Murder which had seemed to be a matter of no moment when it occurred by night in the ditches and prairies beyond the city limits, where it didn't halt any traffic, began to seem personal and dangerous when it was unleashed in the heart of the town in daylight without respect for the rights or lives of the proletariat.

Green hadn't gone far in his study of the record before he saw how greatly things had changed for the worse during his absence. He shared the apprehension of his informed friends over the increasing power and insolence of the mobs. But he was shocked, not so much by the effrontery of the method in the blasting of Hymie Weiss as by its still more incredible consequences.

Capone had come back from Florida and had negotiated an armistice.

16

$200,000,000 A YEAR

THE TRUCE DIDN'T LAST, OF COURSE. NOBODY SEEMS to have expected it would. By implication it remained for years the most disgraceful event of the booze wars. But based as it was on the solemn agreement of Capones, Morans, McErlanes, and crooked officials it held little promise of a useful future. Save as an interesting bit of source material in the expanding history of Chicago in the Federal Building, it was forgotten after April 4, 1927, when "Schemer" Drucci was killed in a detective bureau squad car.

Drucci, according to the official report of his novel demise, was shot "resisting arrest." And maybe he was. But indignant gangsters began to talk about official connivance with Al Capone who, they said, had violated the terms of the armistice by patent subterfuge. The killers got on with their neglected business.

For nearly two years Green and his associates continued

a job that seemed to get more hopeless day by day. Despite the vicious sniping of his rivals Capone had become sure of himself and openly contemptuous of any maneuvers the Federal government might make against him. He had not been able to carry out Torrio's dream of a peaceful monopoly in the beer and alcohol trade, but he had become the strongest individual practitioner in Chicago if not in the country. As the century's leading murderer he was the principal figure in an extensive mythos. He got the admiration of the adolescents and the awed respect of their sycophantic elders. Necessity surrounded him with dramatic mystery. Because of first-hand knowledge about the uncertainty of life he was much in retirement, though seldom alone. But on the occasion of his public appearances he was blatant, bumptious, and — to a large portion of his fellow citizens — insufferable.

At the race tracks in Florida or the ball parks in Chicago his entrances were a matter of gaudy and impressive ritual, like the arrival of Nero at a pageant of ancient Rome. He never merely *walked* into a place. He *swept* into it with a mob of smartly dressed gunmen ahead of him and another at his heels. The simple and appreciative proletariat would stand up to get a good look at him. And in smiling condescension he would wave both hands over his head in a gesture of great good will.

He took no pains to conceal his wealth. He had an estate in Florida and garages filled with expensive cars in Miami and Chicago. He bought $250 suits in dozen lots, silk shirts by the gross. He smiled when he lost literally hundreds of thousands at the races and tossed hundred-dollar bills as tips to waiters and ushers.

by and the little "operations room" in the Federal Building was crammed with the reports of thousands of interviews and investigations and a bewildering mass of calculations. What had been twelve-hour days in the beginning now lengthened to sixteen and eighteen hours with no time off for holidays or vacations. But the work, as the men involved remember it, no longer seemed so hard. For the first time there seemed to be hope ahead.

By this time it is hardly likely that Capone could have been ignorant of the government's interest in his affairs.

The case of Druggan and Lake had been discussed in all the newspapers of the United States, and there was no longer any secrecy about what the Treasury Department hoped to do to prosperous gangsters who had been careless about filing their tax returns. But Capone apparently had begun to believe some of the popular legend concerning his own invulnerability. If he saw danger in the Federal Building, he certainly paid little heed to it as he proceeded with a grandiose plan to complete his dictatorship.

One may pass over some twenty killings in the last two years of his activity. They were too much a part of the hooch trade's workaday routine to merit special mention. Capone's chief annoyance continued to be the North Side mob, on which he continued to work to the exclusion of all other interests but without appreciable result during all that long period. He reached the climax of his career on February 14, 1929, as impresario of a slaughter generally known as the "St. Valentine's Day Massacre," in which most of the leaders of this irritating competition were removed en masse.

George ("Bugs") Moran, currently chief of the mob, had established headquarters in a garage at 2122 North Clark Street. In the office at 11 o'clock on that mild winter morning sat gangsters John May, Frank and Pete Gusenberg, James Clark, and Adam Hyer, entertaining one Reinhart Schwimmer, an optometrist who got a vicarious thrill out of a profitless friendship for the mob, and Alfred Weinshank, another outsider.

As these seven loitered in what one may guess was shop talk, an automobile resembling a police squad car pulled up in front of the garage. Four men in police uniforms came in through the office door.

What happened then is something that, for lack of any eye witness willing to talk about the matter, had to be reconstructed from circumstantial evidence. The four visitors herded the five gangsters and their friends out of the office and into the garage at the point of machine guns, lined them up against a wall, and shot them down.

The murderers were well away before anyone thought to investigate the noise of the shooting. "Bugs" Moran, who arrived at the garage a few minutes too late to be murdered, took one look at the shambles, mumbled that it could have been the work of nobody but the Capone mob, and went into hiding. Fred ("Killer") Burke, a roving assassin with a long record, was later identified as one of the four, but Michigan had a prior claim on him for the murder of a policeman in St. Joseph. So nothing much came of the St. Valentine's Day massacre, except that it marked the end of the North Side mob as an important factor in Capone's marketing problem. The onetime roustabout of The Four Deuces had little to fear from the competition of the remaining mobs. His command of the Chicago situation was unquestioned.

Of course, Capone wasn't in Chicago on February 14, 1929. Oddly enough he was calling on the district attorney in Miami at the very moment when the murder squad was leaving the car in front of 2122 North Clark Street. But he was back in town three weeks later, blatantly aware of his new importance.

Capone's record shows that he was never the brightest mind in the rackets, and it seems likely that the paresis which struck him down in Alcatraz was already working on him. There is something not altogether sane in the plan of the St. Valentine's Day slaughter. And there seems to be no reason whatever in the "victory dinner" at which he sat as host on the night of May 7. Nobody who attended will admit it now. But if one may judge from the newspaper files, the guests included the usual galaxy of gangsters, panders, and public servants. What has been pretty generally established is that three of the merrymakers were John Scalise, Albert Anselmi, and one Joe Guinta described by his friends and co-workers as "a punk."

The bodies of these three were found out on the South Side the next morning, tied up with baling wire and frightfully battered. A post-mortem examination of the contents of their stomachs and a comparison of the result with the published menu of the "victory dinner" indicated that they had taken part in the festivities and had been murdered shortly thereafter. Officially nothing more was ever learned about the case. Unofficially the whole town soon was in possession of all the details. Fully assured of himself, Capone no longer cared much about secrecy. He talked freely to his friends, who in turn seem to have talked freely to anyone who cared to listen to them.

It seems that Capone had begun to doubt the loyalty, if any, of Scalise, Anselmi and their friend Guinta. One version of the story has it that they actually made an attempt on his life, another that they merely were suspected. But at any rate the story goes that they were suddenly grabbed by Capone's bodyguards, trussed with wire, and taken to a convenient cellar, where they were trussed up to rafters. There, in leisurely fashion, "the Big Fellow" beat out their brains with a baseball bat.

The doubtful wisdom of this gruesome procedure came home to him almost at once, for it produced a terrific schism in his own ranks. The murdered men still had friends out in the old Genna territory, and the friends turned out to be unreasonably disturbed. Capone, who three weeks before had been the unchallenged leader of Chicago gangdom, suddenly left town for Philadelphia, where he contrived to get himself arrested and sentenced to one year for carrying concealed weapons.

Over in the Federal Building Dwight Green read the reports of these matters and got on with his work. The end was in sight and such interludes no longer seemed to make any difference.

with the rest of the mobsters." And he turned out to be right about that, although nearly another year went by before he could prove it.

The turn in the case against the absent Capone came late in 1929 when Federal agents, sorting their files for the thousandth time, came upon a collection of ledger sheets for 1925 and 1926 from The Ship and The Hawthorne Smoke Shop, a pair of flourishing Cicero gambling houses. An appended note showed that they had been taken in one of the raids that followed the murder of Assistant State's Attorney William McSwiggin. They had been placed among the records of that case before the start of the inquiry into Capone's affairs and might have been forgotten — as the murder was — save for the accumulation of new masses of documents and the need for space in a filing cabinet.

In themselves the ledger accounts told the investigators little that they hadn't known before, the gist of which was that The Ship had done a business of from $150,000 to $210,000 a week in 1925 and 1926, and in eighteen months had shown a profit of around $500,000. But since the unfortunate McSwiggin had been machine-gunned in front of Harry Madigan's saloon, The Ship had become generally, if unofficially, known as the personal property of Capone.

Here at last was written evidence of revenue that nobody had ever mentioned in a tax return. Half a million dollars seemed hardly worth mentioning in connection with the income of a man who shared the profits of a $514,280,000 annual business. But it was enough to put him into the penitentiary if it could be followed to his pocket with legal proof. It remained only to establish Capone's financial interest in The Ship. So the investigators sacrificed their sleep for another few months.

There have been few manhunts in the history of the Special Intelligence Unit of the U. S. Treasury Department to compare with the one that started immediately after the discovery of the ledgers. Frank Wilson and his agents collected samples of the handwriting of every hoodlum, major or minor, in Chicago. Night after night they compared their exhibits with the fine orderly script in the books of The Ship. And, after weeks of dogged labor, they eventually found a match. A bank deposit slip bearing the signature of Lou Shumway, a former bookkeeper on the gambling house payroll, was written in the same hand as that of the ledger entries. So Wilson embarked on a trail that took him by devious paths from Chicago to Florida.

He found Shumway working for a dog track in Miami and quietly arrested him. The bookkeeper, whom those who attended the Capone trial remember as a shy, inoffensive, frightened little man, took a dim view of the government's plan to remove "the Big Fellow" from the Chicago scene. He had heard about the St. Valentine's Day Massacre, and he knew all about the reported motivation of the slaughter of Scalise and Anselmi. But he hadn't much choice. He could co-operate quietly and with complete protection, Wilson informed him, or he could submit to public arrest and risk Capone's willingness to eliminate a dangerous witness. So Shumway decided to co-operate. He

raiders found no evidence of gambling or other vice at The Ship, The Hawthorne Smoke Shop, or any of the other Capone resorts.

But the Rev. Mr. Hoover wasn't content to let it go at that. He went to the state's attorney and asked that some policemen be assigned to him without preliminary instructions.

"If they don't know where they're going, they can't tell anybody," he said. "I'll tell them what the objective is after they start."

The state's attorney agreed to this unusual plan. The pained cries of the populace since the Lingle murder had been getting too strong to be ignored. So, in due course, the Rev. Mr. Hoover and a squad burst into The Hawthorne Smoke Shop to find such amusements as roulette, chuck-a-luck, craps, and faro in full operation.

There was wild turmoil, of course. The croupiers, stick-men, and bouncers roared at the police in great indignation while the distressed customers milled about in front of the barred exits.

What was the meaning of this outrage! What gave a lot of flatfeet the idea that they could buck the syndicate! There'd be a lot of busted coppers for this night's work!

The noise got so loud that it reached the living rooms upstairs; presently there appeared a large, oily, scarfaced man with pajamas under his suit, whose angry threats rose high above the rest.

"Get out of here," he roared. "Get back to Chicago before something happens to you. I pay plenty for protection and I'm going to get it." Everybody on the premises seemed to know who the angry man was except Mr. Hoover, and Mr. Hoover took the trouble to ask.

"Might I ask," he inquired politely, "who you are and what is your interest in all this?"

And the scarfaced man, who by this time seemed on the verge of apoplexy, told him.

"I'm Al Capone!" he said. "And I own this place — so what?"

In which strange fashion the case against Al Capone was completed. The government never had any difficulty thereafter in proving who got the profits from Cicero's gambling.

Capone may have been bright enough to realize the seriousness of his error, although in view of his subsequent actions it seems hardly likely. He got another inkling of what might be in store for him almost immediately thereafter when young Mr. Green sent his brother Ralph to the penitentiary for three years. But he doesn't seem to have taken that much to heart either.

"I'll beat this rap," he told a reporter who found him in an expansive mood one day at a local ball game. "It's just one of those things — they accuse me of everything."

— 18 —

THE END OF A MOBSTER
AND AN ERA

So, on october 6, 1931, alphonse capone came to trial before U. S. District Judge James H. Wilkerson in the Chicago Federal Building for violation of the income tax laws.

It was one of the biggest days ever seen in a local Federal court with thousands of people trying to get in, guards liberally scattered through the corridors, and a sieve of secret agents to eliminate possible troublemakers at the courtroom door. Reporters from all over the English-speaking world were crammed into the impromptu press quarters in the hall leading to the judge's chambers. The streets outside had seen no such assemblage of moving-picture cameras and newspaper photographers since the first Armistice Day celebration. It was a stirring recognition of the importance of the man who for ten years had run the town's secret government. And Al Capone loved it.

The End of a Mobster and an Era

He came out of his armored car in Clark Street beaming like a matinee idol, or a returning military hero in front of an appreciative public. He spoke loudly and cheerily to friends, real or fancied, whom he saw over the shoulders of the policemen who watched over his path across the sidewalk. He lacked the impressive entourage of young men in pearl-gray hats who used to accompany him to the Miami races and similar events. But somehow he contrived to reproduce his old sweeping entrance with such understudies as the government had provided. He strode into the courtroom, sat down, and looked about with as much interest as his sullen, immobile face was ever likely to show.

His outward appearance was that of a bored ward heeler waiting for the curtain of an opera in which he wasn't interested and whose plot and denouement he knew in advance.

Probably there was reason for his attitude. He had underestimated the seriousness of the situation. And his preparations for looking after himself as he frequently looked out for other people in courtroom trouble had been dangerously delayed. But when the syndicate finally got started with the job it was done thoroughly. Somehow Capone's efficient intelligence department had got hold of the names of the venire from which a jury would be selected to try him. Willing workers had gone out in squads across the town to interview these prospects and make sure of their friendliness with gifts, cajolerie, and threats. So when "the Great Dictator" took his place before Judge Wilkerson's bench he looked upon the advent of the first panel with the superficial interest of a producer observing the work of competent stage managers.

Looking back over the trial and its weird developments, the business of convincing the venire seems to have been only a matter of academic importance anyway. It was chiefly significant as a demonstration of the thoroughness with which the mob, starting late and against unforeseen handicaps, had tried to plug all the holes in their chief's sievelike defense.

One reason Capone had underestimated the seriousness of the situation and had too long delayed preparations to look after himself, was because his attorneys originally had no intention of letting the case get to a jury. After the grand jury voted true bills, the attorneys had received assurances from sources hitherto believed reliable that a deal had been made with U.S. Attorney George E. Q. Johnson whereby "the Big Bugaboo" would plead guilty and the government would recommend a sentence of two and one-half years in a suitable penitentiary.

Nevertheless, considering the facts available to him concerning the venire in Judge Wilkerson's courtroom, Capone's complacence on that October morning of his spectacular public appearance seems to have been amply justified.

Dwight Green, getting ready to start upon the greatest lawsuit of his career, was just as serene and self-confident as his protagonist because he had the advantage of more complete information. Word that Capone's representatives were putting out feelers toward a compromise in exchange for a plea of guilty came to him early in the summer while "the Big Shot's" delinquencies were still taking up the time of the grand jury. Then, shortly after the voting of true bills, he had been summoned before Wilkerson.

Capone had been named in two indictments, one charging him with conspiracy to violate the prohibition act and listing hundreds upon hundreds of separate offenses; the other a less spectacular bill dealing with his criminal evasion of the income tax law. Both of these documents were lying on Judge Wilkerson's desk as Green came into the room. The Judge seemed to be irritated.

"Sit down," he said a bit gruffly, and for a long time he pored over Scarface Al's staggering chronicle of booze and murder.

District Attorney Johnson had concentrated most of his efforts on the prohibition case. Oliver Pagen, expert on such matters for the Department of Justice, had been brought in from Washington to draft the indictment. It was a beautifully detailed and convincing bill and Judge Wilkerson, who also had heard of the suggested compromise, became increasingly angry as he approached the end. When he had finished he threw it across the desk to the young special assistant and demanded:

"Did you have anything to do with this?"

"No, sir," replied Green, "I did not. I have been working only on income tax evasion and drafted the indictment in that case with Assistants Cassius Poust and Jacob Grossman. I know nothing at all about the prohibition case."

The judge made an impatient gesture and leaned forward.

"Well," he demanded, "what does the income tax matter amount to? What kind of case have you got?"

Green suspected that Wilkerson's ire had been aroused by Capone's effrontery in seeking Government sufferance in the face of his record. But he found no reason to take it to himself.

[151]

"I think we have a good case," he said. "And I think we can prove it."

"All right," said the judge, still indignant. "If you think you have a good case you'd better start getting your evidence, because in any event you're going to have to go to trial with it."

Dwight Green up to that moment might have been excused for listening to the talk that Capone would plead guilty and for slowing up his work on a case that would never be heard in court. But an ultimatum was an ultimatum. He knew what he had to do and he did it day and night during the hot months of July, August, and September. He was no longer under any illusions concerning Judge Wilkerson's estimate of the importance of the job he was doing.

During those hot summer months Dwight Green's own estimate of the job he was doing was increased when Capone came into court to be arraigned with the smug anticipation of pleading guilty and getting off with a sentence of two and one-half years. Capone pleaded guilty all right but he did not get off with the comparatively light sentence he had anticipated. This time he had misjudged the situation.

"It is an impertinence," Judge Wilkerson said in effect, taking cognizance of the reported deal, "for anyone to attempt to make suggestions to this court or to presume to make binding agreements limiting the court in the exercise of its judicial functions. The court will tolerate no interference and if this defendant wishes to enter a plea of guilty it must be free from all conditions. . . ."

Quickly Capone's attorneys petitioned the court for

Federal Prosecutors Green (left) and Samuel Clawson (center) watch Al Capone make a $50,000 bond. His power smashed by Green, Capone starts to prison shackled to petty auto thief (center) and U. S. Marshal Laubenheimer.

U. S. Attorney Green (right), Special Assistants Salter (left), and Harness inspect a truckload of Insull case exhibits. Before being brought to trial, Insull found temporary refuge in Greece.

permission to withdraw their client's plea of guilty. The petition was granted July 31.

In addition to all this highly relevant knowledge of Judge Wilkerson's attitude, which he possessed on the morning of October 6, young Mr. Green was armed with most of the facts concerning the mob's defense strategy, including the attempt to fix the jury. Like Capone, whom he surveyed with an untroubled eye across the lawyers' table, he was not much worried about it — but for a different reason. Green knew in advance what Capone's counsel were still to learn — that whatever the utility of the suspected venire it would have no further place in the proceedings.

Two weeks before the date set for the trial, the Treasury agents had come in with evidence of what the mobsters were about — evidence that included names from the supposedly secret jury list on which they were working. District Attorney Johnson, his assistant, Green, and Agent Frank Wilson had taken this material to the Judge. And the Judge, unperturbed, had completed his arrangements.

So the first surprise of the case came a few minutes after the opening of the trial. And it was produced so quickly and quietly that only the defendant and his attorneys showed indication that it was a surprise at all.

The veniremen had been herded into the front seats temporarily reserved for them when Judge Wilkerson, black-robed, calm, and inscrutable, took his place on the bench. Normally the selection of the jury would have commenced at once, and Capone was looking quizzically at the four men on the end of the first row as if trying to guess the nature of the gifts his boys had provided for them.

But there was a slight variation in the proceedings. The Judge called his bailiff and without preliminary comment or explanation gave an order.

"Take this entire venire to Judge Woodward's court," he said. "And bring his venire to me." So all the men who had been the object of the mob's solicitude arose en masse and were escorted out of the room.

To most of the spectators all of this looked like a minor bit of court routine. But at the lawyers' table Dwight Green looked at Capone and smiled. Capone leaned over the shoulders of his lawyers busily studying a list of names and scowled. The elimination of a receptive jury that he didn't intend to use might have been an insignificant reverse. But his counsel didn't like it. Albert Fink and Michael Ahern were smart and resourceful and experienced, and they could read the signs. This was going to be one case in which the old methods weren't going to work. Neither of these talented attorneys found much to smile about from that moment until the verdict was in.

The new venire arrived and selection of a jury was begun. The job was finished the same day. On the morning of October 7 Dwight Green outlined the government's case to the jury and the trial proceeded to its inevitable conclusion.

Shumway came to identify the ledger sheets of the Cicero gambling houses and to point to Capone as the man who had employed him. He was a bit nervous, as one who knew the mobs as well as he did had every right to be. But he ignored the threatening glare in Capone's eye and made a good witness.

Ries, the messenger, took the stand to tell of how he had

sent the cashier's checks to Capone in Miami. And he, too, seemed to have lost all fear of consequences. Capone listened stolidly, apparently bewildered at the thought that a cheap hireling should thumb a nose at him.

It was a black moment for "the Big Bugaboo" that presently became blacker when Wilson arrested his bodyguard and close friend, Phil D'Andrea, for carrying a gun into the courtroom. Judge Wilkerson wasted no time on D'Andrea. He interrupted the hearing only long enough to sentence him to six months for contempt of court and see him start to jail.

"D'Andrea's a damn fool," observed the defendant, and that was his last coherent comment on the trial. Apparently he still had hopes of being saved by some eleventh hour miracle — otherwise his unwillingness to believe the final verdict would not have been so obvious. But for the rest of the hearing he sat slumped in his chair, scowling at the jury and mumbling unheeded orders into the ears of his lawyers.

With Hoover and bank tellers and telegraph messengers and dozens of little people "the Big Shot" had never heard about, Dwight Green built up an overwhelming case. Defense counsel winced when the correspondence file of Tax Expert Mattingly's efforts toward a compromise were read into the record. "The Big Shot", the Great Intelligence of popular legend, had blithely admitted his delinquencies in writing. Day by day the Capone of the folk tales faded, and in his place appeared a new Capone, the real one, who was basically gullible and fuzzy-witted and generally contemptible.

This picture was presented to the jury in a summation that seemed hardly necessary. Dwight Green had done his work in the marshaling of the case and presented his best argument through the lips of witnesses. The jurors expressed their approbation by convicting Capone on five counts of the indictment.

Nobody who sat through that long day is likely to forget its climax. The case had gone to the jury at 2 o'clock on the afternoon of October 17, 1931, but the wrangle over the verdict had dragged along for hours. When 6 o'clock came and no decision had been reached, Judge Wilkerson went out to dinner. The defense attorneys and their prize hoodlum walked out through the deserted corridors of the Federal Building obviously cheered by the delay. In the now disordered courtroom an unprecedented assemblage of newspapermen, telegraphers, and spectators lolled about in boredom making bets on the outcome — and when the Judge came back at 7:30, a considerable number of the boys were offering odds on an acquittal. Minute by minute Capone's prospects got better until the moment when the foreman signaled an agreement with an ominous rap on the jury-room door at 10:54.

Capone, summoned from the Lexington Hotel, arrived at the Federal Building fifteen minutes later, flustered and mopping his brow. He entered the courtroom with Messrs. Fink and Ahern, took off his topcoat, sat down, and attempted to conceal his excitement.

Judge Wilkerson came back to the bench, an austere study in black and white. The courtroom quieted for the first time in more than nine hours. The tired-looking jurymen filed back into the box. The judge turned to them.

"Gentlemen, have you reached a verdict?"

"We have," said the foreman, and the others nodded assent.

Clerk James O'Sullivan took the verdict from the foreman's hands and began to read it in a booming voice. . . . .

"We, the jury, find the defendant, Alphonse Capone, not guilty on indictment 22852 ——"

Capone sat up quickly with a broad smile. He beamed his congratulations on his poker-faced attorneys. Everything was going to be all right. He was still the big boss, and he was going to beat this case as he had beaten all the others. Meantime O'Sullivan's voice was rolling on loudly and impressively. Presently it bored into Capone's dim consciousness and his face fell ——

". . . on count one of indictment 22853, guilty. . . ."

He'd been too early with the cheers. Count four was a felony rap carrying a penalty of five years in the penitentiary and a fine of $10,000.

". . . . on count five, indictment 22855, guilty. . . ."

Capone began to crumple in his chair. Count five was another felony. He stared at O'Sullivan as the recital went on.

". . . . on count nine, indictment 22853, guilty. . . ."

Another felony!

The hoodlum, obviously crushed, did not seem to hear the remaining findings of guilty on counts 13 and 18 which accused him of misdemeanor in failing to file income tax returns for 1928 and 1929. He was gazing in bewilderment at the grim face of Judge Wilkerson, where even a lout of his limited intelligence could have noted the signs that marked the end of the road.

The Judge lopped six years off his possible seventeen years' stay in the penitentiary by making the sentences on counts one and five and 13 and 18 to run concurrently. The incidental fines still totalled up to $50,000, and the costs of prosecution assessed by the court came to another $50,000.

There were some preliminaries to the sentencing. . . . . The defense attorneys entered a motion for a new trial, went into brief conference, and withdrew it. They asked for a stay in judgment and were over-ruled. Fink and Ahern were two of the shrewdest men in criminal law practice in Chicago; as they turned their valuable client over to the deputy marshals, they seemed satisfied with the result of the trial even though Capone, obviously, was not.

In their calm acceptance of the verdict, they paid young Mr. Green the tribute of extremely competent critics. Like all of those who had watched the unfolding of the trial through two tense weeks, they realized that his greatest accomplishment, even more than the sending of Capone to Alcatraz, had been the deflation of "the Big Bugaboo." Green had been right in calling him the symbol of public evil, rather than a great menace in his own right. He had come into a sort of brevet rating as the country's Number One gang leader through the stupidity and connivance of smart men more evil than himself. The lout from Five Points who had been touted as a genius of crime was shown to have been just a lout. Witness after witness had piled up evidence, not of his ruthlessness but of his innate and unchanging stupidity. Confronted by an honest prosecutor and an unreachable judge for the first time in his life, he had been as helpless as the trussed up trio whom he beat to death with a baseball bat.

He was as dead as Hitler long before his hurried and unimpressive funeral in Chicago in 1947. When he went out of the Federal Building, handcuffed to deputy marshals and raging at photographers, he had already ceased to exist. And with his passing went the hold of the gangs on Chicago. A system that couldn't save so widely advertised a chief as Scarface Al could never again hope to nullify local government and make a comic spectacle out of the courts.

The people who had been permitted to see the truth through the practical eyes of Mr. Green went home that night aware that they had surrendered their inalienable rights to a false face. The strength of gang rule had been nurtured by the senseless fears of its victims and might have gone on forever, save that a gullible thug from Brooklyn had tried to take in too much territory.

former returned to the District bench, and eventually retired; Johnson stepped down and went into private practice, while a deserving Democrat took up his judgeship.

But the New Deal in Washington made no move regarding the United States attorneyship, temporarily held by Dwight Green; so the judges of the District Court met together and appointed him to the job. Obviously, he was the best man available, just as obviously he had earned it; and, once again obviously, the New Deal agreed — maybe reluctantly — on both counts. Green was not particularly anxious to take the job, but the judges persuaded him that it was his duty to do so; these were turbulent times, the great Insull crash was headed for its aftermath in Federal courts; and who, the judges argued, was better fitted to battle with this multi-million-dollar tangle than Dwight Green?

He agreed finally, reiterating his reluctance, admitting that it was his duty; it took three years before he felt that he could shake off the responsibility. He had been in office barely two months when the Insull mess was dumped in his lap.

The Insull case involved billions of dollars, thousands of stockholders, hundreds of thousands of business transactions, and uncounted headaches. It was a case that required months of intensive study, and careful and exhaustive investigation. It was a case that always seemed to involve more dollars than sense.

Sam Insull had been one of the richest men in America. His personal fortune was estimated at anywhere between one hundred millions and one hundred and fifty millions.

He was on the boards of 85 tremendous corporations, and president of the board of most of them.

His empire, built of utility companies and holding corporations, extended through 37 states, and represented a working capital — according to the most reliable figures available after the wreckage — of approximately four billion dollars.

That is, one day Sam Insull was a mighty multimillionaire and his empire was a formidable organization. The next day Insull was a fugitive, and his empire was little more than a prairie, full of prairie-dog holes.

The great companies organized and developed by Samuel Insull were in receivership. Investors in thirty-seven states were crying "thief." Creditors were rushing into the courts to start suits for damages. Lawyers were everywhere, trying to pick up the pieces. And every law-enforcement and crime-detection and crime-prevention unit in the Middle West was considering immediate investigations.

After the shock had worn off, and after the panic had begun to subside, and while everybody was investigating everybody else, a curious change was noticed in the attitude of many of the citizens.

They began to express a sneaking admiration for Samuel Insull, and to voice a pity for him in the collapse of all his ambitious projects. Even some of those who were hardest hit in the crash of the Insull properties were heard to say it wasn't all Sam's fault.

Maybe it wasn't.

Sam Insull had come to Chicago, indirectly, from his native London. He had served for some years as secretary to Thomas A. Edison. He had helped Edison organize and float some of his early electric companies. He had proved himself something of a business genius, and had been sent to Chicago to nurse the Edison Company there.

He came to Chicago in 1892 to find the local Edison Company one of several small concerns. Its capital was less than one million dollars. He went to work — as he had worked for and with the wizard of Menlo Park. He worked 18 or 20 hours a day — not, however, at the salary of $50 a month, which Edison had once paid him. He built a large central power station. He secured more efficient methods of distributing light and power. He made more things hum than the dynamos. His company began to outstrip all its competitors.

In 1907 he was able to induce all his rivals to consolidate with his firm and thus formed the Commonwealth Edison Co. And, when the papers were all drawn up and signed and properly witnessed, there was Sam Insull in the president's chair.

Next he went after the power companies and utilities outside Chicago, organizing the Public Service Company of Northern Illinois. In 1912 he had made a collection of utilities outside the city and state, organizing the Middle West Utilities Co.

He put the Peoples Gas, Light, and Coke Company, on its financial legs, and taught it how to walk properly. Yes, he became president of that concern too. Then he took over the Chicago Elevated Lines, and the electric railroads going out of the city to the north, the west, and the south. He formed holding companies, naturally, and interlocking directorates. There was hardly anything he didn't do that could be done to keep the empire strong, and growing. He even made political contributions now and then — and now and then was criticized for so doing.

For forty years the name of Insull was a magic name in Chicago and the Middle West. It meant just what the name Midas meant centuries ago — a man who turned to gold everything he touched.

Perhaps, though, King Midas never had so many friends as Samuel Insull. He had thousands of friends — and more than a thousand, it was once charged, were on his preferred list. That was supposed to indicate that they were given advance information on stocks, or were permitted to buy certain stocks at much lower prices than less preferred friends. He had many friends, but few intimates.

In his happier days Sam Insull lived like a king — a rich king. He was a king. He had a ten-room penthouse on the roof of the Civic Opera Building — which, incidentally, he helped to erect. He had a 4,445-acre farm just south of Libertyville, Illinois, about 40 miles from the Chicago Loop. He put an Italian villa on this place, spending a few score thousands of dollars on the architectural plans and construction, and several more score thousands on the "scraps" of furniture that went into it.

He had 62 employees at Libertyville, and he built schools for their children. He also helped to build a number of churches in the near-by communities. Any pastor within a hundred miles of his farm, no matter what his denomination, could touch Sam Insull for a few thousand dollars most any time. And people in and around Libertyville used to say they used Insull light and power, sent their children to an Insull school, banked in an Insull bank, played golf on an Insull course, rode into Chicago on an Insull train — perhaps to work in an Insull office — went to an Insull church on Sunday, and, when sick, went to an Insull hospital.

Insull traveled much, and leisurely. He was almost as well known in New York, and London, and Paris, and other great cities, as he was in Chicago. He lived many weeks at a time in England, and had a country house and farm near the village of Theale. He also had a little resting place in New York which he used occasionally.

Insull might have kept control of his empire — and that empire might have been twice as big now as it was then — had it not been for the big crash in Wall Street in 1929, and the great "Depression" — people still speak of it with awe — which followed.

He might have stayed in control of his empire if he had tried to retrench. He did not retrench; instead he expanded more than he wished to, because he was afraid that Eastern capital had designs on his empire. He whipped his cohorts — and himself — into a very frenzy of buying. He and his intimates bought Insull stock at any price — and kept on buying it. The Eastern sharpshooters laughed and kept on selling.

Insull's idea was to keep the market strong for all his securities, and to retain control. Thousands and thousands of admiring Chicagoans thought he was right. And they went along with him, to the extent of their buying ability.

Then — *puff!* A wind blew from the East. And that was that.

Fabulous Sam

They tell the story of the mighty Sam Insull visiting the office of Owen D. Young, in New York — "coming with his hat in his hands" — and asking Young and a group of other Eastern capitalists for an extension of credit. There was a loan of $600,000 involved — a trifle Insull couldn't manage to pay. Would the Easterners wait a little longer? They went into Young's office, leaving Insull outside, to consider the matter.

Then they came out, and Insull put down his dollar cigar, carefully, and stood up to hear the verdict.

He was then $27,000,000 in the red. He had 600,000 investors depending on him and his 85 great corporations. He had perhaps a thousand cities, little and big, in the 37 states of his empire, also depending on him — and his gaining the help of these Eastern financiers.

Mr. Young looked at Mr. Insull with sorrow.

"Hopeless?" the latter asked.

"Hopeless," the former answered.

"Receivership?"

"Receivership."

Insull picked up his cigar, to show that his hands were steady, and puffed it a moment in silence. Then he said, "I wish my time on earth had already come," and walked out of the office.

He went back to Chicago. He managed to be appointed receiver of his bankrupt companies. Charles A. McCulloch, of the Continental Illinois Bank, was named co-receiver.

But this situation did not continue long. It ended shortly after McCulloch began to look over the books of the Middle West Utilities Co.

Martin Insull, Sam's brother, was president of that corporation. Sam had brought him from London, educated him, developed him into something of a businessman, and given him his high position.

McCulloch ousted Martin as president, and, as he later testified, "denied him even a day's salary." He swore that in all his career he had never seen such gross mismanagement and inefficiency as he had found in the affairs of the Middle West.

There was only one man in all the Insull wreckage that McCulloch had any use for. That was Samuel Insull, Jr. McCulloch was lavish in his praise of Insull's son. "He's a fine boy," he summed it up, "and he's been carrying the whole load of the disaster on his own shoulders, without whining."

Insull retired from all his companies — and was voted a pension of $21,000 a year by the four biggest of them. He was in Europe when the news broke that the Insull empire was lost, and overrun with creditors and "cops"; everything was in chaos.

Sam Insull was in Paris, and Martin was in Canada, when United States Attorney Dwight Green was instructed by the Attorney General of the United States to look into the four-billion dollar smashup and determine whether or not the government had reasons to indict and prosecute.

John A. Swanson, Cook County's state's attorney, threw himself headlong into action while the city was still shaking; and before many weeks had passed he had secured indictments charging Sam and Martin Insull with embezzlement, larceny, and larceny by bailee.

Crowds of hurt and bewildered and frightened stockholders were forming committees, in a piteous endeavor to

=== 20 ===

THE INSULL CHASE

CHICAGO WAS CHAGRINED OVER THE INSULL INCIDENT, but not unduly resentful. It is a tremendous city, with a tremendous tolerance for the weaknesses of its notables. It had borne with the gangsters in the golden Prohibition days — even boasted a little of the gangsters' wickedness. It chuckled a little at the unseemly greed of the "Gray Wolves" in the City Hall itself. It forgave J. Ogden Armour when he went broke — although he caused a lot of inconvenience. (Armour, the packer, lost a million dollars a day for a hundred days, shortly after the First World War — and stocks were a little wobbly for a time.) It was ready to forgive Sam Insull.

Naturally there were hundreds, even thousands, of small investors who loudly said they would like to see Insull brought back so that they could tar and feather him and then put him in jail to rot. But they did not represent the bulk of Chicago's citizens.

The sneaking admiration the average Chicagoan felt for the utilities' fallen czar, became open admiration when he defied the power of the United States to bring him back for trial. It was a lawless era, perhaps, this era when it was smart to have a bootlegger and to break the law with every drink one took. It was an era when the patriotism worn so devotedly through the war years had begun to get thin and to exhibit the shoddy.

There were thousands who rejoiced that Insull could "get away with it." They said "more power to him." They wished they could do the same. They put themselves in Insull's place, and wondered if they would have grit enough and power enough to defy Uncle Sam as he did. The man became, in a crazy sort of way, a comforting symbol to them.

Perhaps the only man in Chicago who really wanted Insull back in the city was the young prosecutor, Dwight H. Green; and Mr. Green desired the return of the exile not so much as a defendant for trial, but as an expert who would be able to help in unraveling the tangle of affairs he had left behind.

In October, 1932, the Cook County grand jury returned true bills against Samuel and Martin Insull. They charged that Martin, "by means of embezzlement, larceny, and larceny by bailee," had abstracted $377,720 from the treasury of the Middle West Utilities Co., and used the money to protect his personal brokerage accounts.

They charged that Samuel and Martin used $66,000 of the funds of the same corporation to protect brokerage accounts carried in the name of Washington Flexner.

They charged that the brothers took $104,222 from the

Mississippi Valley Utilities Investment Co., to protect brokerage accounts.

And the County Board put up $10,000 for "extradition expenses." Cook County, it seems, confidently expected to get Sammy back without much trouble.

Prosecutor Green made no comments at the time. He was too busy scanning thousands and thousands of papers that might or might not indicate evidence of mail frauds, or violations of the bankruptcy act.

Sam Insull was in Paris when the grand jury mentioned his name. He went away quickly, traveling through Italy into Greece. Greece, at that time, had no extradition treaty with the United States.

The American Embassy was asked to get busy. It did. But nothing happened. Back in Chicago the boys got together now and then and joked about the matter. Sammy, they said, must have brought a lot of grease to Greece. He must have taken five or six millions with him, they said, just for pocket money. Well, they said, more power to the guy.

Washington raged, but Sammy stayed in Greece.

Herbert Hoover, then President of the United States, signed a request for Insull's extradition. It had no effect on the Greeks.

It was not until February, 1933, that Green began presenting evidence to the Federal grand jury. Fifteen agents of the Bureau of Investigation — the now famous F. B. I. — after a six-month investigation directed by their chief, Melvin A. Purvis, had provided Green and his assistant, William J. Froelich, with bales and bales of ammunition.

On February 27th, before Federal Judge Charles E.

Woodward, the brothers Sam and Martin Insull, Sam Insull Jr., Stanley Field, prominent industrialist in Chicago, Harold L. Stuart, head of a brokerage concern, and others, were indicted.

"This is only the beginning," said Prosecutor Green. "I propose to investigate fully all the ramifications of the so-called Insull empire, its creators, and its sponsors."

The indictment contained 120 pages, and was illustrated with photostatic copies of letters and statements sent through the mails to stockholders and investors. There were twenty-five counts in the indictment alleging mail frauds.

Of course, as everybody knows, an indictment isn't proof of guilt even in America. It wasn't proof of anything in Greece.

The Chicago newspapers made much of the news; and Chicago's citizens talked a lot about it. But there wasn't much indignation.

The true bill went into particulars on some counts. For instance it pointed out that investors were told, through the mails, that the yield on the stock of the Corporation Securities Co. — the last company organized by Insull — would be 6% or more, when, "in fact there could be no income on the stock by reason of the fact that the company operated at a loss throughout its existence." The stock advertised as the "best buy on the market," was, according to the indictment, actually worthless.

Those Chicagoans who had always bought "the best buy on the market" — and many times regretted it — said, "So what? So that's the American way of doing things."

The officials of the Greek Court of Appeals, who, in due time, read the indictment and the current request for

Insull's extradition, had no word for it. They shook their heads in seemingly honest bewilderment, and said "we find no evidence of guilt."

"And even if we did find Mr. Insull guilty of mail fraud," one of the officials confided to a newspaperman, "we would have no right to send him back to the United States. We have an extradition treaty now, of course, which, as you know, was forced upon us by American diplomats; but it does not cover the crime of mail fraud. We are so sorry. We can do nothing. Therefore, we must continue to protect that nice American millionaire."

Dwight Green sighed when he heard the news. After all his work! But he had no intention of giving up the fight. He studied the extradition treaty. He studied international laws. He found out that if Mr. Insull couldn't be extradited for mail fraud, or embezzlement, or larceny, or even larceny by bailee, he could be extradited for trial on charges of violation of the bankruptcy laws.

He directed all his efforts thereafter to searching the records for any hint of hidden assets, or clues to kindred crimes. The receivers of the corporations after six months of investigation, reported they had found no evidence of tampering with the bankruptcy act. States' Attorney Swanson had found nothing either, though he said he had searched in that direction.

Dwight Green went carefully over all the bank and brokerage records he could find. So did all his staff who could be spared, and all the trained men the United States government could furnish him. Likewise the prosecutor questioned every Insull executive he could summon, and everybody else who might be able to help him.

In July, seventeen of the nineteen men indicted on charges of mail frauds appeared before Federal Judge J. H. Wilkerson, and pleaded not guilty. The only two who failed to make an appearance were Sam Insull, who was taking the sun in Athens, and Martin Insull, who was enjoying the beautiful scenery in Canada.

In August, Dwight Green, primed with documents, appeared before another Federal grand jury, and secured indictments charging Sam and Martin Insull and others with a number of violations of the bankruptcy laws.

This time, it seemed, the obdurate Greeks would have to comply with demands of the United States for the fugitive.

But the Greeks, the earliest of philosophers, took an extremely philosophical view of the matter. They read this second indictment, and looked quite serious. They debated the matter solemnly. And they reached the natural philosophical conclusion.

"Yes," they said. "It looks bad. Perhaps poor rich Mr. Insull did, technically at least, violate the laws governing bankruptcy. But we cannot believe that he acted in bad faith in not adhering to the strict letter of the law. After all, he was just a victim of the depression."

All legal efforts to return Insull to the yearning arms of his Uncle Sam had failed. So pressure was used through the diplomats, and the Greeks began to weaken. Although it hurt them, they decided to expel Insull from their country — but was it not charitable to wait a more propitious moment? Behold, even now the feeble old man lies in his room, extremely ill. His heart is not good. Perhaps he has not many days to live. When he begins to recover, then of course. . . .

But even as they talked, the "dying" old man was chartering a freighter and making arrangements to skedaddle.

Before the United States authorities were aware of what had happened, Sam had gone to sea. He was somewhere in the Mediterranean, having a grand time, and looking for a good port in which to escape the legal storm.

Chicago began to admire Sam Insull more and more. There was a boldness in him, a grand arrogance, a rich defiance they relished. He might be a feeble old man with a weak heart, but he had spunk enough to fight the whole United States and keep his freedom. So, "you have to hand it to him," people said. "He's a game guy, and I hope he gets away with it."

But nobody gets away with flouting the United States government. And Insull didn't get away with it for more than two weeks after his exit from Athens. He landed in Istanbul. And, before the Turkish government could decide what to do about him, agents of the United States government kidnaped him, put him aboard a New York-bound steamer, and brought him home.

It was May, 1934, when Sam Insull was brought back from Europe, and Martin from Canada. Samuel was held in the Cook County jail — but only for one night — as a Federal prisoner. He was photographed and fingerprinted, just like anybody else.

Then he met Martin — for the first time in nearly two years — in Judge J. F. Fardy's criminal court, where both were arraigned on the state indictments. Both pleaded not guilty. The brothers made no show of emotion when they met. They simply said hello, smiled, and parted.

On May 22, Sam Insull was brought into Federal Judge Philip L. Sullivan's court on the Federal indictment.

Through one of his battery of lawyers he declared that he had been shanghaied from Turkey, illegally brought to Chicago, and therefore the court had no right to try him.

Prosecutor Green leaped to his feet to answer that.

"Insull is here," he cried. "The court is not concerned with the means of bringing him here." He cited cases of other kidnaped prisoners who were convicted and sentenced. Some had been taken out of foreign countries in direct violation of treaties, without extradition papers of any kind, but it had never mattered to the courts who tried these men. The only fact that mattered to the Judge was that the prisoner was arraigned before him.

Judge Sullivan sustained him in this; and then the fight began to fix bond, pending trial. Green demanded it be fixed at the sum of $200,000 — the highest bond ever asked in a case of this kind.

"This case is one of great public importance," he said. "It involves the loss of many millions of dollars. The Government does not want this prisoner to escape again, which he might attempt unless the bond is fixed sufficiently high.

"His going away at a time when he must have realized his services would be needed to settle his corporations affairs was suspicious at least. When he was ordered to leave Greece, he disguised himself by dyeing his hair and mustache and penciling his eyebrows. He slipped out of an apartment where he was supposed to be confined by illness, chartered a steamship, and set sail out of Athens. The purpose of this disguise was to perpetrate what I submit was an escape. He later bragged about how much smarter he was than the police who hunted him.

"No expense was spared in preparing his defense; and large sums were undoubtedly spent by the fugitive in his attempt to escape. It has also cost the United States government a great deal of money to bring the fugitive here, and to prepare to try him. Therefore every precaution should be taken to insure his safekeeping."

Insull was already under bond of $50,000 to answer the State charges. Defense attorneys mentioned that. But Judge Sullivan sided with the prosecutor. Bond was fixed at $200,000.

Sam Insull pleaded not guilty, a day was set for his trial, and he went to a room in St. Luke's Hospital "to gather strength for the ordeal that faced him." He occupied a "charity room." But then, in his palmy days, he had given many thousands of dollars to the hospital. He was getting only a little of his own back.

Insull remained in St. Luke's quite a little time, "a poor sick old man persecuted by the Government" — and thousands of people, some of whom had lost all their savings in the crash of the Insull empire, sent him letters and telegrams of sympathy. They bade him have courage. They assured him he would be vindicated. They congratulated him on his "heroic fight" for freedom. And they asked how they could help him in his troubles.

Dwight Green made no comments. He worked harder than ever to get ready for the trial.

=== 21 ===

WE GAVE THE BEST WE HAD

THE TRIAL OF SAMUEL INSULL AND HIS CO-defendants, opened on October 2, 1934.

Counsel for the aged tycoon told the court that Mr. Insull had a very weak heart, and the excitement of long trial — especially if his friends were tried with him — might have disastrous results. The trial of a group would, naturally, produce more excitement, more confusion, more witnesses, more attorneys, and would, of course, take much more time, than the trial of one defendant.

Dwight Green had anticipated this objection, and was ready for it.

"Mr. Insull may have a weak heart," he told the court, "but I am ready to prove by the testimony of eminent medical witnesses, who have had the opportunity to observe the defendant's health, that he is in much better physical condition than he was when he arrived. His stay in

Chicago has done him a lot of good, and he should be able to stand whatever rigors there may be in a long trial.

"Then too, Your Honor," he added, "there is this to consider: These men operated together in the transactions that led to their indictment; they were indicted together; they should be tried together.

A separate trial was denied Insull. Prosecutor Green opened the Government's case with a two-hour talk to the jurors, in which he outlined the evidence he would present.

"You will find, gentlemen," he said, "that some of the testimony to be offered here will be pretty dull. There are thousands of entries that must be brought to your attention, entries in the books and records of the corporations. It will be a long, slow, tedious process. It will be rather monotonous and uninteresting. However, through these entries, we will show the scheme that was used to defraud thousands of victims, to unload millions of dollars in worthless securities on the public. There will be many witnesses and voluminous documents; yet we will show there was a simple conspiracy to swindle, cheat, and defraud the public.

"The specific charge in this case, which charges mail frauds, concerns the sale of $143,000,000 in securities in the formation of the Corporation Securities Co., and its intricate setup of subsidiaries."

Listening to that part of his address, one got an idea of the long, monotonous, tedious, dull, and uninteresting hours spent by the young prosecutor in poring over the various entries in the corporation books, in the bank and brokerage accounts, and in the letters, pamphlets, and circulars mailed to investors all over the country by the defendants. He had spent more than a year in the study of these papers, and in the questioning of witnesses.

Green was well aware of Chicago's sympathy for Samuel Insull — a mawkish pity which was never so well displayed as it was during the public auction of Insull's furniture and personal possessions.

Great crowds of people streamed into and out of the Civic Opera Building during the sale of the Insull belongings in the ten-room penthouse. It cost each one of them a dollar to attend the sale; but that didn't deter them. Some of them came with lunches and thermos bottles of coffee or iced tea or lemonade.

Most of them came not to buy, but to look around, to peer out the windows — from which on a clear day one could see as far as Oak Park to the west, or to the shores of Michigan to the east — to ride up in Insull's private elevator, paneled in walnut and red damask, to touch his four-poster bed, complete with tester, and bedspread of rose and gold brocatelle, to finger his tortoise-shell brushes, or to tell the folks at home, later, about the big table in the dining room, a monstrous bit of furniture that would accommodate 24 diners, about the refrigerator that would make more than 200 ice cubes at a time, about the carpets, the rugs, the brocades, the paintings, the antiques, and especially about the silver and crystal bathroom.

It was stated in the newspapers of Chicago that the furnishings of the penthouse were worth $100,000 at the very least. They brought less than $26,000 at the auction.

The same phenomena of human curiosity about the rich, and human sympathy for the dethroned and bankrupt, was observed at the sale held at the Libertyville farm, in the New York apartment, and at the estate in England.

The people who journeyed out to Libertyville made a somber picnic of the affair, tracking through the house to see all there was to see, visiting the barns to view the blooded horses and cattle, tossing rinds of sausage and crusts of bread to the proud swans — or throwing them into the goldfish ponds — trampling over the flower beds — and buying as little as they could for as low a price as they could. There was also a four-day auction in the New York house.

Even those most bitter toward Insull softened when they read of all his financial troubles. He had ruined a lot of people; but he had certainly ruined himself also. Perhaps he suffered more than anyone; for, to have a fortune of $100,000,000 or more, and then to lose every cent of it and be so much in debt you've got to sell or hock all your Aubusson rugs and other doodads — man, that is really tough.

The one thing needed to make these people actual champions of the man was the advent to Chicago of Mrs. Helen Coyinzoglu of Athens, Greece. She had been hostess to Mrs. and Mr. Insull during most of their stay in Athens, and she came to Chicago for the express purpose of knicking her ex-guest for $60,000.

"Because I took care of him during his exile, when he was sick and persecuted and hunted," she said, "he gave me some gold watches, encrusted with jewels, and a number of diamond shirt studs. He also told me that he was making a will that would leave me $20,000. When he left Greece, Mrs. Insull asked me for the studs and the watches, saying she was going to put them in a safe place — in a vault in the Morgan bank in Paris. I want that jewelry, and I want the money promised me. I went to a lot of trouble for Mr. Insull — keeping the newspapermen away from him was a big job in itself — and I am not asking for anything I am not entitled to."

The woman departed from Chicago shortly, without the watches or the studs. Mr. Insull's lawyer, and the chief of his battery of defense attorneys, former Judge Floyd E. Thompson, made the statement that her intended suit had been settled by the payment of $4,000 to her.

Dwight Green knew that pity for Insull might outweigh all the testimony to be presented against him, and all the arguments he and his associates could offer for conviction. But there was nothing he could do about it.

The trial took eight weeks. It cost the government over $100,000. And it was estimated, it cost the defense approximately $150,000. More than two million words were written into the record during the forty-five "working days" of the trial. Eight of the most prominent lawyers appeared for the defense. Mr. Green was assisted by Special Prosecutors Leslie E. Salter and Forest A. Harness.

Mr. Insull took the witness chair in his own defense on November 2d, nine days before his 75th birthday, and, prompted by the questions of his counsel, told the story of his life from the time he was a clerk in London, paid at the rate of five shillings a week — $1.00 — until the day he pleaded not guilty to the indictment.

It was a fascinating story he told, the story of a poor boy's rise to enormous riches and power — and his fall. He sold the story to the jurors — and sold himself with it — with the ease and eloquence he used in selling his securities. He made each man of the jury believe in him, even as he had made the biggest men in America believe in the strength and integrity of his corporations.

He did not hide the fact that he had helped to make the Chicago Opera Company a superb organization, that he had helped — with money and advice and precious time — to erect the magnificent edifice now standing at Madison Street -and Wacker Drive — the building on which his penthouse perched. Nor did he hide the fact that he had helped thousands and thousands of Chicagoans, and men and women in other cities, to something like financial independence.

Gradually his lawyer led him into the mazes of finance, his development of small companies into gigantic industries, his phenomenal empire building, and then, at length, his determined and frenzied efforts to save that empire despite the depression that "swept throughout the world" — to save the empire and the savings of the 600,000 men, women, and children, who owned stock in it.

Insull kept saying, every little while:

"I would do it again."

It was like a battle cry. It roared defiance — even though uttered in a quiet voice. It got under the skin.

Special Prosecutor Salter questioned Mr. Insull after he had finished his story on direct examination.

Insull, who had been a nice, benevolent, persecuted old gentleman while he spun the story of his life, showed now that he could be overbearing, arrogant, disdainful, and even angry. He answered some of Mr. Salter's questions with insolent replies, and challenged him again and again with the loud cry:

"I would do it again."

There was no escaping that refrain. Spectators repeated it outside the courtroom. Reporters tossed it back and forth among themselves. And the jurors? Of course nobody knows exactly how they reacted to it, but perhaps it had as much effect on them as on everybody else.

Insull had taken a four-billion dollar loss on the chin — and he'd take it again, if he had to, so long as he was convinced he was right.

Nobody knows how the average juror thinks, how he feels about the prosecution's side, or the case for the defense, what he thinks of the various witnesses, or the judge. And certainly nobody knows what twelve different men think about the same thing. So it would be silly to say that the jurors thought this or that — or that they thought at all.

They went through the eight weeks of the trial, giving no indications whatsoever of their thoughts about the case — if any. Sometimes, especially when the testimony was dull and uninteresting, they seemed bored and sleepy.

But, when the case was ended and the judge's instructions had been finished, on November 24, 1934, they took only two hours to reach their verdict.

They found Sam Insull and all his co-defendants not guilty of using the mails to defraud.

One of them explained later to newspapermen that he and his fellow jurors had felt all along that Insull and his friends were not men of "criminal intent."

"They were merely victims of the depression," he said. "They may have used bad judgment, and probably did. But they were honest. They did the best they could — and they went down with all the others. I hadn't been a juror in this case very long until I was convinced these men were not guilty."

The newspapermen then asked Mr. Green how he felt about it.

Green, with a smile, told them.

"I have no comment to make, except to say that the Government presented its case carefully and in all its details. We gave the best we had in us."

22

INSULL FADE-OUT

SAM INSULL EMERGED FROM THE MAIL FRAUD TRIAL
as something of a hero. Thousands of letters and
telegrams of congratulations poured in on him
and Mrs. Insull in their suite at a North Side hotel. The
corporations which had considered canceling his $21,000
pension, reconsidered the matter.

Nobody pinned a medal on him; but many people took
pains to show how they felt. Some months after the trial
the Chicago Opera Company sent him a key to the front
door of the "opry house," in token of "keen appreciation of
what the opera-loving people of Chicago owe you." The
U. S. Board of Tax Appeals relieved him, his wife, and
his son, of approximately $70,000 in Federal income tax
claims. And several university presidents — including a few
who had conferred honorary degrees upon him in his untroubled day — wrote that they had always had confidence
in him.

Dwight Green watched the victorious old man and his friends leave the courtroom, and thought of all the days and nights he had worked to decide in his own mind whether or not they were guilty, and then to see that justice had its fling.

Was this justice? Twelve American citizens had decided that it was. There was nothing the prosecutor could do but bow to their decision.

Still the matter wasn't settled. The indictment charging violation of the bankruptcy act was still hanging over Insull's head. There were also the State indictments to be considered. Insull might yet be found guilty and sentenced.

Green was not distressed by the outcome of the trial. He had simply done his duty. He had done it well. He had lost, but in the knowledge that he had given his best, he did not feel himself a loser. A man who works hard and conscientiously and in the sincere belief that he is in the right, may be defeated, he considered, but he cannot be beaten. He has gained something in the fight that is more valuable than any victory — and has retained his own integrity.

He ate his Thanksgiving dinner with as much relish, and as deep a feeling of gratitude to Heaven, as did Insull himself.

In March, 1935, the Insulls were victorious in the criminal court of Cook County. Sam Insull's defense was pretty much the same as it had been in the mail fraud trial. And his reiteration of "I would do it again," had the same effect.

It was rumored, after this trial, that Prosecutor Green was recommending that all further charges against the defendants be dropped, but Green would not say whether the rumors were true or false.

He took no part, however, in the trial on the bankruptcy charges. He had submitted his resignation as United States Attorney, and was staying in office only until his successor should be appointed. He was a Republican in a Democratic setup — and he had plans for a future that would not be connected in any way with a Democratic administration.

The bankruptcy trial began in June, 1935; but it didn't last very long. Judge John C. Knox, sitting in Judge Wilkerson's court, directed the jury to return a verdict of not guilty.

The directed verdict marked the end of all Insull's adventures with the law. The remaining charges against him and his relatives and friends were nolled; and he was free again — to do what he wished, go where he pleased.

For a year and a half he lived quietly, with Mrs. Insull, in a three-room apartment in the Seneca Hotel. And then, one day, very quietly, he joined the army of those who had had and now had not, those who had been and now were not. He faded quietly out of Chicago life, and went back to Europe. He was not exactly broke. He was still receiving $21,000 a year. And he was not without influence or friends.

He spent some lazy months in London, visiting the scenes of his boyhood, stopping at hotels where he had once entertained dukes and barons and counts and prime ministers and movie stars, and spending a little time at the cemetery at Putney Vale, just outside the metropolis, where his mother and father had been buried.

He visited Paris again. And there, in July, 1938, he died.

He dropped dead as he was purchasing a ticket at a subway station. He fell flat, smashing his glasses, and cutting and bruising his face. He was taken to a hospital, and left there for a few hours. The attendants were not greatly concerned about establishing his identity. He could not possibly be anybody important, for all the money he had in his pockets was thirty francs, the equivalent of 84 cents!

They were concerned about him only when they found, in his billfold, a receipt made out by his hotel for the laundry. There was his name, his magic Midas name.

The body was taken to England and placed in that little cemetery at Putney Vale, close to the remains of those who gave it birth.

In August his will was filed in the Probate Court in Chicago. It left the estate, valued at $1,000, to the widow. The will was executed June 14, 1932 — the day Insull had given his creditors two million dollars in cash and prepared for the long exile that was to end with his flight from Greece. It listed $14,000,000 in debts.

Sam Insull had faded out at last.

living, his days spent at the work he loved, his evenings in his home or in the homes of his intimates. But this was not to last.

On a sunny winter afternoon in December of 1938, a group of men called on Dwight Green in his law office. They were important men so, despite the fact that he was busy on a brief, he told his receptionist to usher them into his office.

"You have a fine war record," observed their leader, Barney Goodspeed, treasurer of the Republican National Committee. He gazed with interest at the office walls, which were hung with the original drawings of newspaper cartoons. He gazed at the young man behind the desk. He gazed at his fellows.

"And you have a fine civic record," he continued. "For both these reasons, or either one of them, and for your outstanding character, and for the ability you have shown, we think you should run for Mayor."

"That's right," chimed in Silas Strawn. "You can serve your city in peace as you have served your country both in war and in peace."

Sewell Avery and A. W. Harris signified their approval.

Green was forty-one. He had been nearly twenty years away from the war, and from thoughts of the war. He hadn't tried to "cash in" on his war record. The idea had never occurred to him. He didn't intend to milk that record now for any dividends of honor or position.

And then he was waited on by a delegation of World War I veterans: these were George Sugarman, Thomas A. Patrick, David L. Shillinglaw, Dwight Anderson, William

M. Devine, Emmet F. Byrne, and Frank H. Collins; all were presidents or past presidents of veteran organizations.

There was something more than touching in this group of old war buddies coming to his office and urging him to be a candidate. It meant that they would be with him in another fight, helping him bear the burdens of a difficult campaign; and it was good to have friends who would fight for you in peace even as they had fought in war.

He liked the idea of being Mayor of Chicago. There was so much he could do for this great city, he knew. There were so many things Chicago needed! But he wasn't going to do anything in a hurry. No good soldier rushes into battle without some idea of the enemy's position, without as much necessary equipment as he can carry with him, and without some hope of victory — a hope based on reason, not on emotion.

He had been pledged the support of nearly all the fifty Republican ward committeemen. They wanted him, they said, "because there is a popular, genuine, and insistent demand on the part of the citizens for young, new, liberal, and vigorous leadership in the Republican party."

They chose him, they added, "because we believe you have the character and ability to provide such leadership."

They had let him know, incidentally, that a sizeable campaign fund was being raised.

The 46th Ward Regular Republican Organization, led by Judge Oscar F. Nelson, had been especially insistent in its call on him.

"It is essential," said the resolution of this organization, "that the Republican party nominate for Mayor a man of

executive and administrative ability, a man of youth and
energy, a man of proven integrity and experience in public
affairs. The 46th Ward has a resident in Dwight H. Green,
who possesses all the above qualities."

Judge Nelson and Charles S. Dewey, who had been
mentioned as potential candidates for the mayoralty, vol-
untarily withdrew in favor of the former prosecutor. And
many other public figures made it clear that he was the
first choice of the G.O.P. — if he wanted the nomination it
was his.

The way was clear. But Green wanted to know, before he made up his mind, what the Republicans of Chicago
thought of him — not the ward committeemen, or the
aldermen, or the judges, or the others in command of the
party, but the rank and file of the voters.

And when he began to hear from them he decided to
fight.

The campaign began shortly before Christmas, 1938;
and the candidate made a characteristic talk.

"The city government," he said, "should take a more
active and progressive part in the development of air
industry. It should consider aviation problems from the
civic instead of the political viewpoint. Men in the profession know there is no reason for Chicago ever to take
second place to any other city as an air center.

"If I am elected I propose to work hand in hand with
these men. I will not allow an administration of mine to
foster political interference in so important a matter. I
will guarantee the co-operation of the city government in
all movements designed by airmen to make Chicago the
supremely great air center it can become."

Another subject that affected the candidate deeply was the problem of youth.

"Chicago's future," he declared, "demands the development of outlying areas and the provision of more opportunity for our youth. There is a real need for protecting and encouraging our citizens of tomorrow."

The early months of 1939 were, perhaps, the busiest months of his busy life. He paused, during the strenuous campaign, only long enough to celebrate his 42d birthday, at a dinner given him in a Loop hotel. He was constantly in motion, conferring with party leaders and with delegations from wards, neighborhoods, trade unions, and other organizations, making speeches, touring the city, and sleeping now and then, whenever there was nothing else to do.

He went at the job as he had gone at every other job offered him, with all his energy, with all the resources of his mind and nerve and will, and with all the strength in his body.

It was a different sort of job than any he had known. It differed vastly from the work of hoeing corn, pitching hay, stacking wheat, and other boyhood chores. It differed vastly from the job of carrying newspapers along a daily route, or driving a truck for a lumber company. It differed too from the job of quarterback on the college football team, from teaching fellow soldiers to fly, from practicing law, and from prosecuting offenders of the law.

Yet, it seemed to him at times, there was something of all his other jobs in this business of running for Mayor. Was he not cultivating the political soil, getting ready for a bumper crop of votes? Was he not delivering the newspaper of himself along a route that embraced every bailiwick in Chicago? Was he not driving the truck of the Republican party? Wasn't he carrying the ball for dear

Let's Go!

old G.O.P.? Wasn't he soldiering again with his buddies? And, in his many talks, was he not upholding law and order, and doing his best to rid the city of lawlessness?

His platform was a simple "declaration of purpose."

"I will completely eliminate politics from the school system and the police and fire departments, and will rigidly enforce civil service in the selection of personnel," he said.

"I will appoint members of the Board of Education whose character and experience will insure that the funds for educational purposes will be used to give Chicago the best school system in the world.

"All contracts and purchases will be on a competitive price basis. No applicant for a position will have to pay tribute to any person or organization, and no conscientious employee will be in danger of losing his job because of political influence.

"I will eliminate politics from the administration of relief; and, by the suppression of racketeering and the reduction of taxes, I will endeavor to induce new industries to come to Chicago to provide additional jobs for our citizens.

"I will work unceasingly for adequate relief for the aged and needy.

"I will destroy the political influence of the criminal element in the government of our city, and I will completely divorce crime from politics."

In the primaries, Mayor Edward J. Kelly was re-nominated as the Democratic candidate. Green increased the tempo of the campaign. Kelly was a shrewd campaigner. He had been years in power. His machine was efficient and far-reaching and was well entrenched. And it was operated by men who played marbles for keeps. The machine had snowed Kelly's opposition "deep under" in the primaries.

"Landslide for Kelly," said the headline of one of Chicago's dailies, issued on the day after the primaries.

"Landslide for Green," said another.

Something like one million two hundred thousand votes had been cast for the six Republican and Democratic contenders in the race. Mayor Kelly had received more than half the total.

States Attorney Thomas Courtney, runner-up in the Democratic race, had promised to go along with the winner. That meant that Kelly would have much more support than he needed to win the forthcoming election — unless Green could rally a tremendous Republican army from those who had not voted in the primary and also win some of the Democratic forces to his banner.

Green did his best to win adherents away from Kelly.

"The Kelly-Nash machine," he wrote precinct captains, "spent $2,500,000, and used every method of pressure and purchase in the primary. Nevertheless, 1,220,000 registered voters failed to vote for Kelly. They await our call to follow the new leadership for Chicago."

If the Republicans could secure that army of non voters, or a great percentage of them, Green might yet be elected Mayor.

"It will be done," Green said.

That phrase became the fighting slogan in the mayoralty campaign.

It was an exciting and an amazing fight; but, on the morning of election day, April 4th, it was clear to almost every political expert in town that Green had "not a chance."

Mayor Kelly was re-elected. He received more than 820,000 votes.

But Green, who hadn't been given a chance by anybody, polled the astounding total of 637,107! That was a larger vote than any Republican candidate for any office had received in the previous ten years. It was more than three times the vote he had received in the primaries.

It was a Democratic victory.

But it was a Republican triumph. A new star had been discovered in the political skies.

The leaders of that party were jubilant — and optimistic about the 1940 prospects. If they had only worked as hard as Green, they realized — too late — they could have beaten Kelly. Well, they would work hard next year, and the year after. The Republican party was coming back strong.

A few months later Dwight Green announced that he would start campaigning for the Republican nomination to the office of Governor of the State of Illinois. He felt he owed it to those 637,107 Chicagoans to keep fighting — and on an even bigger front.

= 24 =

GOVERNOR OF ILLINOIS

O N HIS FORTY-THIRD BIRTHDAY, JANUARY 9, 1940, Dwight Green's headquarters for his guber- natorial campaign were opened in the LaSalle Hotel, Chicago; the theme song of the reception — which lasted four hours — was, "Happy birthday, dear Guv'nor, happy birthday to you." The decorative motifs for the guests were green Green buttons and green Green carna- tions — sort of off-season St. Patrick's Day. Newspaper reporters estimated the crowd which milled in and out of headquarters, jammed the lobbies, and spread into a score of lesser receptions in private suites at more than five thousand people.

Not all of these were from Chicago. "Downstate" — which means in political Illinois-ese, anything outside of Cook County — was well represented by dyed-in-the-wool Republicans who had come up to look over this entry — a man whom few of them had ever seen, but of whom they had read much: his prosecution of gangsters, his conduct of the Insull trial, and his extraordinary showing in the recent mayoralty race against Edward Kelly and the soundly entrenched Chicago Democratic machine. They looked him over, they talked to him, and he thawed them into a preliminary friendliness which was, later, to develop into wholehearted support.

Former State Representative Richard J. Lyons of Libertyville, popular with the downstaters and particularly so with his ex-colleagues in both houses of the legislature, was running against Green for the nomination. Lyons seemed to have the lead; Green's strength, said the political prognosticators, lay only in Chicago — and Lyons, they opined, would get enough votes in the city, added to his downstate strength, to put him over.

Dick Lyons had been laying the groundwork for his campaign since he had retired from the legislature in 1938 to run against Democrat Scott Lucas for the United States Senate; he lost a hard-fought contest, but his first battle had committed many leaders throughout the state to support him in his next one.

Dwight Green did little talking about his chances of winning; he was too busy getting acquainted — and campaigning. He thought he had a good chance but he was doing no boasting; he realized that he had to sell himself to the strangers downstate — and he also realized that Dick Lyons was no stranger to those folks. It was a clean, decent campaign, waged between two clean, decent men, each of whom had a wholesome, respectful regard for the other.

There was no mud slinging; Dwight Green did not fight that way — and neither did Dick Lyons; nor did they permit their campaign helpers to use dirt. The basic trouble in the Republican party in Illinois these many years had been factionalism, the methods of leaders who had put personal ambition ahead of party success and public welfare. Leslie (Ike) Volz, one of Governor Green's two present-day administrative assistants (the other is Don Hyndman, former Associated Press bureau head in Springfield), rolled the sins of past Republican leaders into a short and compact indictment, tracing the gradual decline of party power through a factionalism which, occasionally victorious, was sapping its own "innards." Mr. Volz began his study of Illinois Republican politics when, as a youth of nineteen, he was engaged as secretary by the late Fred Lundin, "the poor Swede," that extraordinary political character who first made "Big Bill" Thompson Mayor of Chicago.

"Take the various party leaders over the years," said Mr. Volz. "Lundin, Deneen, Crowe, Thompson, Harding, Small, Brundage — all of them factionalists — all of them thinking of themselves rather than of the party. Such selfishness was bound to have the result it did. When a faction leader got in, the other faction leaders were out, out of patronage, out of jobs. We were out of luck till Green came along; and we were lucky that the Governor's primary opponent was Dick Lyons — a man who was also above petty factionalism."

Even in Chicago, where Dwight Green had shown his marvelous vote-getting abilities in his fight with Mayor Kelly, matters did not look too rosy at the start of the gubernatorial campaign — that is, they did not look too rosy from the purely political point of view. Forty-three out of fifty ward leaders were for Lyons; twenty-five out of thirty Cook County township leaders were for Lyons. But Green had learned something in his mayoralty campaign; as a practicing politician he was still a tyro but he had faith in the people. Running against Kelly he had polled an extraordinary vote from a party that had come to be considered moribund in Chicago — a vote that had been gathered in the teeth of the machinations of one of the smoothest, most efficient organizations that ever came to function in American political history.

He went to the people. He did not ignore the politicians but he had two sound campaign managers in the persons of John P. Dempsey in Chicago and John Brown, a Kansas (Illinois) farmer downstate; both were doing good jobs of promotion and organization. Green liked people; in the old days when he was a Federal prosecutor he liked to talk to juries made up of all sorts and types of people — cross sections, they were, of American folks. He used to watch these juries as he talked to them and when he was getting close to them, when his words were making an impression, he could generally tell it; he was then, is today, and always will be, a good judge of people.

So that was it. He went out and talked to the people — not windjamming, not highfalutin — just ordinary sound common sense, presented in simple, understandable words. He was asking the people for a job and he wanted the people, rather than the politicians, to give him that job.

He was untiring in his journeys through the state; it was not unusual for him to appear in ten different towns in one day. In the little places he frequently arrived unannounced, calling on the local leader, introducing himself, seeking for permission to present to the people his request — that he be appointed their principal servant in Illinois. The representatives of labor listened to him, liked him; women listened to him, liked him; youngsters heard him, noticed that he did not talk down to them, that what he said was easy to understand; and thousands of war veterans, remembering that he was one of them, paid heed to his easy flow of words, told their buddies that here was the man.

Philip Kinsley of the *Chicago Tribune*, now taking a well-earned rest after forty years of toil and considered one of the greatest of living reporters, had this to say of Dwight Green a few days before the close of the primary campaign:

"As a campaigner Green is not a backslapper. He is quiet, reserved, deliberate in speech and action, dignified and serious — too serious, some of his friends say. But he has a warm handclasp — a direct look into the eyes — and makes a good personal impression. And he has gone almost everywhere in Illinois during the present campaign, up and down the main streets of the little Illinois towns, calling on the butcher, the grocer, the barber, the tavern keeper, the garage man, the banker, the newspaper editor, as well as appearing at political meetings day after day and night after night. It is hard work, but he has thrived on it."

Kinsley interviewed Green on primary election night — when, by a smashing plurality, he became the Republican nominee for Governor — and wrote of him:

"Mr. Green has come through the campaign in splendid health. His eyes were clear, his hands steady, as he looked over the early returns. However, he was tired, and said so."

[206]

He was tired, but he rested only a little while; then he plunged with all his vigor into the fight to make 1940 an outstanding Republican year. He was campaigning now, not only for himself and those on his slate; he was also working to elect Wendell L. Willkie president of the United States.

Dwight Green, with no previous political experience, was astute enough, just as soon as he knew he had won his party's nomination, to go to those leaders of his own party who had opposed him in the primaries and to ask them, man-to-man, for their support; he did not have to go to Dick Lyons, for Dick came to him. But there were some others who hung back, remembered the old days of factionalism which had come so near to actually destroying the Republican party in Illinois.

"What's the use?" they argued. "He has no time for us. If he does win by some chance, he'll remember we were agin' him."

Green talked them out of that way of thinking, just as he had talked so many men on the street, by the roadway, and on the village corner into his way of thinking. He had dire need of these men and women if the party was to break its record of eight years of failure to acquire any state political office. He wanted a team pulling together, and he talked to them in the football jargon he knew so well. He recognized their right to disagree as between two individuals such as himself and Dick Lyons; but now they were after something bigger — a team, united and pulling for a victory of the party — no longer a matter of victory of one man over the other. They came over — en masse —

and today the Governor of Illinois counts among his closest friends and supporters men who did all they possibly could to defeat him in that first gubernatorial primary.

Dick Lyons appeared at the Illinois State Fair, in Springfield, in the summer of 1940, in the white trailer he had used so spectacularly in his campaign against Green. But there was Green's name painted on it instead of his own, with the names of Willkie and McNary (the Oregon senator who was the G.O.P. vice-presidential candidate).

"Dick Lyons rides again!" his friends shouted. "Now we know Green will be Governor."

"I'm going to campaign for Green harder than I ever campaigned for myself," said the state's best loser. "Brothers, watch my smoke!"

Dick Lyons' ride produced much smoke. And there were many other riders. The smoke was so thick it could be noticed all over the United States. When it subsided — and the opposition conceded defeat — a happy but weary Republican Governor-elect found he had beaten his Democratic opponent, Harry B. Hershey, by 256,000 votes. He had carried with him into office every major state candidate with the single exception of the secretary of state. For the first time the people of Illinois had approved the presidential candidate of one party but had chosen the Governor from the opposition ticket. It was a personal triumph for Dwight Green.

25

LEARNING A NEW TRADE

Inauguration of illinois' new governor on january 13, 1941, was a memorable event. Republican leaders insisted on that. The Governor-elect had little flare for ceremony and, from the habit learned in his career as a lawyer and prosecutor, he was immersed in preparation for the biggest case of his life. But he cheerfully went along with the inaugural plans, although he insisted to his friend, Ferre C. Watkins of Chicago, who was the general chairman of the event, that state expenditures should be held to the minimum.

The State Armory was crowded for the formal ceremony at noon when Tito Schipa sang and the Governor delivered his inaugural address. It was even more crowded in the evening for the grand ball where the Governor and his lady greeted a milling throng of dancers and then returned to the Executive Mansion to shake hands with added hundreds.

To Dwight Green the high light of the day was when he placed his hand on the Bible presented by the Reverend Archibald J. Carey, Jr., Chicago Negro churchman, and repeated after Chief Justice Walter T. Gunn the oath of his office. And the most convincing tones heard in his almost hour-long inaugural address came as he declared:

"Certain basic principles . . . indispensable to the preservation of free institutions . . . have guided my approach to the specific topics in this message.

"Those principles are: first, uncompromising honesty and integrity in government; second, strict economy and efficiency; third, co-operation between labor, industry, agriculture, and all other elements in our economic life; fourth, the freeing of the people from machine rule and political despotism. These are the principles to which our administration is irrevocably dedicated. Upon them all our plans are built."

The next day Dwight Green took up the job of applying these principles to the administration of the state government of eight million Americans. When he arrived at the Capitol from the Executive Mansion, he just followed the crowd to the Governor's office, which he had never before seen. There, his state-police chauffeur literally had to shove a passage through the crowd of friends, curious spectators, and anxious job seekers. The Governor shook hands with many, waved to others, entered the private office, sat down at the big desk.

The responsibilities entailed in the possession of that desk were very different from those of any other position he had occupied. He was now the chief executive of a public business which spent more than $225,000,000 a year.

Thousands of men and women employed in the Code departments directly responsible to the Governor were engaged in such divergent tasks as building, maintaining and policing the state highways, caring for more than 43,000 wards of the state in the hospitals and institutions of the Public Welfare Department as well as some 12,000 inmates in the state's penal institutions; they inspected the factories, the mines, and the dairies of the state; they operated state parks, game preserves, and fish hatcheries; they supervised public utilities and administered the workmen's compensation laws; they administered the very important programs of the Department of Public Health; they licensed and supervised the operation of barbers, beauticians, undertakers, and a score of other licensed trades; they administered the old-age pension and relief funds; and among many other things they collected the state's taxes and distributed many millions of dollars to county, city, village, and school district officials. And, as the Governor was to be reminded many times, the people who were both the clients and the stockholders of this great business were going to hold him personally responsible for each detail of its operation.

In addition, the General Assembly was in session. It was his duty under the Constitution to advise and consult with the legislature and to approve or veto its enactments. By common practice it was his obligation to assume leadership of his party's legislative program if it were to succeed; and by political necessity he had to keep enough of the 204 members happy so as to insure the adoption of appropriation bills and other measures essential to the accomplishment of the plans he had outlined in his inaugural message.

The legislators were disposed to be very friendly with the new Governor. They felt that he needed their advice and they had a deep conviction that, particularly if they belonged to his party, they had by virtue of their office the right to drop in on him at any time and stay as long as they liked.

A change of administration always causes turmoil and unrest in any state capital. That turmoil and unrest was magnified in Springfield in January, 1941, by the fact that the state's finances were badly strained and that the capitol was undergoing the second change of leadership in a little more than three months.

The cold facts as to finance were that there was only a little more than one million dollars in the General Fund of the State Treasury. The appropriations for old-age pensions and general relief would be exhausted before the end of the month and, unless emergency appropriations were obtained, these State services could not be maintained and payrolls could not be met.

The financial troubles were heightened by events which had taken place in Springfield shortly before Governor Green took office. Governor Henry Horner had died early in October, and had been succeeded by Lieutenant Governor John Stelle. Horner and Stelle were both Democrats — but they belonged to different Democratic factions; they had been the principals in a bitter personal political feud. The advent of Governor Stelle had been the occasion for the resignations of most of the department heads and lesser administrative officials under Horner. During "the hundred days," as the Stelle regime had come to be called, the State Government had been run by men new in their jobs who knew their rule was to be short-lived.

Thus the job to which Dwight Green sat down that winter morning was very different from preparing and trying a lawsuit. Yet the new Governor already had a grasp of it. In the ten weeks since the election he had been training for it harder than he had ever trained for anything else in his life. He knew that success in public office depended on competent performance by assistants given a free rein in the execution of their assignments. He had appreciated the freedom of action he had been given by his superiors in the Capone case, and he had determined to find men to whom he could trust the administration of the key positions under him.

In the selection of his aids he consulted freely with Republican leaders, because he recognized both his obligation to them for their support in his election, and the fact that an effective administration would require their continued support. He consulted freely with the newspapermen whom he had found to have a keen and impartial understanding of the details of state government. He consulted with many of the applicants for those positions, and with those he had personally asked to consider becoming applicants. Yet he made his own decisions and kept his own counsel, and the announcement of the names of his Cabinet almost overshadowed any other news of the inauguration.

Newspapermen who analyzed the appointments found that in some instances the Governor had called upon the services of men who had held similar posts under previous Republican administrations; in others he had rewarded active party leaders both in Chicago and downstate; in still others he had chosen men with whom he had been closely associated and in whom he had great personal confidence; and in one instance had renamed a director of the previous Democratic administration, who had been a career man in his department.

This appointee was Dr. Roland R. Cross, who today is still director of the Department of Public Health. Rodney H. Brandon, named as Director of Public Welfare, had held that position under Governor Emmerson, last Republican executive. Robert M. Medill had been Director of Mines and Minerals under Governor Lowden way back in 1917. Walter A. Rosenfield, Director of Public Works and Buildings, and Frank G. Thompson, Director of Registration and Education, had ample experience in public and private business to qualify them for their appointments; they also had been active leaders in Republican state politics for many years.

Howard Leonard, the Director of Agriculture, was a veteran agriculturist who had been active for years in Farm Bureau organization and the work of the Illinois Agricultural Association. The Director of Labor, named at a time when the rivalry between CIO and AFL was becoming most intense, was Francis B. Murphy, a downstate businessman who had started as a coal miner. Livingston E. Osborne, a leader in amateur sports and the Izaak Walton League, was the new Director of Conservation. The Director of Insurance was Paul Jones, a Danville lawyer whom Green knew well, both from association in veterans' organizations and from the fact that Jones had held appointment under President Hoover as United States Attorney for the Eastern

District of Illinois when Green had held the same place in the Northern District at Chicago.

Perhaps the appointment which received the most attention from the press and caused most discussion among professional politicians and lobbyists was that of George B. McKibbin as Director of Finance. McKibbin, a wealthy Chicago lawyer, was known most for his activity in the Y.M.C.A., the Civic Federation, and other organizations — civic and philanthropic. He had occasionally been active in Republican politics, and bore the reputation of being a "reformer." He had become interested in the civic possibilities of the election of his fellow alumnus of the University of Chicago as Governor of Illinois, and had been an ardent Green supporter — but with no thought of taking any personal part in the administration. Green appreciated these facts; he also appreciated McKibbin's knowledge of taxation matters. He knew that the Director of Finance, with his supervision of the state budget and state purchases was a key man in any state administration. He knew that every director of finance was the subject of attack, just or unjust, and that the Governor's Director of Finance, like Caesar's wife, must be above suspicion. Green decided McKibbin was the man for the job; he may have been the first, but he was certainly not the last man to be persuaded by the Governor to accept an appointment which promised grief far beyond its rewards in cash or glory.

McKibbin first agreed to accept the place temporarily. He stayed almost five years, during which the State worked itself out of the red and accumulated a cash reserve which he carefully husbanded for permanent state improvements. In the meantime he effected a reorganization of the entire state services and a reclassification of employees which provided for equal pay for equal tasks throughout the various departments of the State Government. He became the Republican nominee for Mayor of Chicago in 1943; with Green's backing he came even closer to beating Kelly than had the Governor in 1939.

How well Green, with no previous experience in state administration, had judged the men he chose for his first Cabinet was shown by the fact that seven years later five of the original department heads were still serving. And T. P. Sullivan, his original appointee as chief of the state highway police, was Director of the Department of Public Safety, a new department in which the state police was merged as a part of the Governor's legislative program in that first session.

Another interesting item in his first appointments of important state commissions was the inclusion of Valores J. Washington on the Commerce Commission and William E. King on the Industrial Commission. These were the first Negroes named to serve those bodies in Illinois. Washington, a brilliant editor and publisher, remains a member of the board which regulates the railroads, bus lines, and local public utilities of Illinois; King, a former state senator, is a member of the Commission which administers the workmen's compensation system.

With the aid of these lieutenants and with the traditional co-operation of the legislature in all "honeymoon sessions," the new administration negotiated its immediate hurdles without mishap. The emergency appropriations were passed; State expenditures were held down to an absolute minimum, with the result that payrolls were met on time and the State's complete solvency was maintained.

The General Assembly accepted the Governor's recommendations for reduced expenditures for the next biennium, and the budget adopted was smaller than the State's expenditures in the previous two years. For the most part he got along well with the legislature. His program for the creation of a separate Department of Public Safety to consolidate the state police system, the operation of the State's penal institutions, and the regulation of pardons and paroles — which had frequently given rise to scandals in Illinois — was enacted into law.

However, he ran into some snags. One was on the Republican campaign pledge to take the sales tax off food. The issue had first been raised by Richard J. Lyons, Green's unsuccessful rival in the primary. It had been written later into the Republican state platform by the state convention. As a lawyer Green was aware of the legal difficulties involved in exempting any class of retailers from the State's sales tax, which technically, to meet the provisions of the State Constitution, was a retailers' occupational tax. When he found that the party's pledge could not be carried out without a Constitutional amendment, he proposed the submission of such an amendment to the voters and obtained the necessary legislative action to do so.

The amendment ultimately was defeated by another technicality — the provision that an amendment to the Illinois Constitution must receive the affirmative vote of a majority of all the electorate voting for members of the General Assembly. At the statewide election of 1942, the affirmative votes for the amendment exceeded the negative votes by more than ten to one, but still fell short of being a majority of all votes cast for the legislative candidates.

Meanwhile Green contrived to give to the housewives of Illinois a savings comparable to what would have resulted from removal of the sales tax on food. At the time of the 1940 campaign, the retailers' occupational tax amounted to three percent of all sales — three cents on the dollar. The law which created the tax had provided for a tax of two cents on the dollar — but subsequent legislatures had levied an extra cent for the next biennium. All the calculations for the elimination of sales tax revenue from food had been based on the assumption that the three-cent rate would be continued on all other items.

It was estimated that the elimination of the tax on food would result in a reduction of sales tax revenues by less than one-third. Therefore the Governor decided not to ask for a renewal of the three-cent rate but to make up the loss caused by the greater reduction in revenues which would thereby result by imposing a tax on cigarets and increasing the state liquor taxes. As a result, on July 1, 1941, the Illinois' retailers' occupational tax automatically reverted to two cents. Despite the extra burdens and increased costs of State Government in the war and postwar years, Green steadily refused to consider suggestions that the retailers' occupational tax be restored to its previous higher rate.

The Governor met another snag and learned about legislatures in the defeat of the Schnackenberg Bill. This measure had provided for a legislative investigation of the finances of the various local governments in Cook County which were coming to the legislature at each session for relief from their problems of inadequate revenues due to increased expenditures and delinquency in tax collections. The Democrats bitterly opposed the bill as a party issue. Ultimately it was defeated in the House when a few Republican members from Chicago decided it was more to their advantage to vote according to the dictates of the Democratic Mayor in the City Hall than to follow the recommendation of their Republican Governor.

By July 1, when the Assemblymen went home at the completion of the regular session of the Sixty-second General Assembly, the new Governor had firmly mastered his job. The administration had been rescued from the brink of insolvency and was on a sound financial basis. The new executive had won the confidence and respect of Senators and Representatives and had strengthened his popularity with the people. The problems of patronage which had closed in on him the night of his election were still pressing, and the machinery which he had set up to screen applications for employment was still grinding — grinding too slow to suit the politicians, but grinding surely to see that the deserving Republicans chosen for State jobs were also qualified to perform them.

Dwight Green had learned a lot about state government, and about human nature, and he had accustomed himself to a new routine of living. He had learned to spend most of his days at the State House seeing the vast army of men and women who "have to see the Governor," and to spend most of every night in long sessions at the Mansion when the real administrative work was accomplished. He had become a great listener, as patient and as poker-faced as any judge before whom he had ever argued. His keen mind, his experience with witnesses on the stand, and the hours of reading and study few knew about, helped him to sift the wheat from the chaff. An occasional remark or significant question often convinced his visitors that he was learning about the State of Illinois faster than they had expected — sometimes, faster than they liked.

He had learned, too, to accustom himself to another side of the job as Governor. He found that the people of Illinois, as in many other states, expected their Governor to lend the blessing of his official presence to all sorts of civic affairs — the dedication of a new bridge or highway, the celebration of the centennial of a village, or a testimonial to an outstanding citizen in any walk of life. He accepted as many such invitations as was humanly possible, because he liked people, and because it gave him a chance to talk to and rub shoulders with the inhabitants of all sections of the state. He found himself jumping from one section of Illinois to another, traveling even more than in his election campaign.

To the travel necessary for these appearances, he decided to add a visit in person to every state institution, every state park, every outpost of state government. He was determined to acquire first-hand knowledge of the whole vast state plant which he had been hired to manage. It was strenuous, but he liked it; particularly when he could feel that the state activity he was inspecting was making life easier, or more worth while for the people.

He continued to spend as much time as he could with his friends in Chicago, where he maintained an apartment, but he found he liked living in Springfield, where his two daughters were established at school. He chafed a little at the restriction which the office of Governor imposed on his informal habits of living. But he had long since grown used to having his job interfere with what he would like to do. In the Army, in the newspaper office, in his Federal tax work and in his succession of big trials, he had become accustomed to working while other people were asleep or enjoying leisure.

Those intimates who saw Dwight Green at close range and vowed as a result that they would never want to be governor, never heard him being sorry for himself. Those who warned him that he was pursuing a man-killing pace were later confounded as they watched him grow ruddier and stronger while the gray hairs spread quickly from his temples to the rest of his head.

girls go and do your homework. You won't get any better marks in school because you're the Governor's daughters."

Back in 1925 when Dwight Green was about to leave for Washington, a young woman whom he had occasionally escorted in Chicago said to him, "I know a beautiful girl in Washington. I think you'd like her. Why don't you call her when you get down there; I'll give you her phone number. Her name is Mabel Kingston."

After the young attorney got settled, he telephoned. Miss Kingston was delighted to hear from him but she was sorry, she couldn't see him that week. Like all pretty girls of the twentieth century, her date book was filled. Young Mr. Green telephoned again, and again young Miss Kingston was sorry. But this was the same Pete Green who had called out the Ligonier volunteer fire department at the age of four, who had become quarterback of the Wabash football team, and who time after time had bounced back to the *Examiner* city room after Howey or Carson had fired him. He telephoned still again. Miss Kingston invited him to call Sunday afternoon.

Dwight Green slicked himself up for his date and hailed a taxicab. When he arrived at Miss Kingston's residence, he told the cab driver to wait. The call lasted twenty to thirty minutes. "Hmmm," thought Mabel Kingston, "he's either very wealthy or he's trying to make an impression." She soon learned he was not wealthy.

Before the call ended, Dwight Green discovered one of Miss Kingston's tastes and one of her traits. "I don't like spats," she said with characteristic frankness, pointing to her caller's necessary adjuncts to a male fashion plate of

1925. The next time Dwight called, to escort Mabel to one of the many dances that marked his courtship, he did not wear spats. He has not worn them since, except on most formal occasions.

After the Greens returned from their honeymoon, the bride learned that she had acquired not only a husband, but a culinary problem. "He was the world's most difficult man to cook for when we were first married," she reminisced years later. For Dwight Green, as many other midwestern boys reared in small towns, was strictly a meat-and-potatoes man.

Mrs. Green — who knows good food, likes to prepare it, and enjoys eating it — decided that Pete, as she called him before the children were born, was missing too many dietary delights. She embraced a cause of the kind in which she, and every other woman who is essentially a home-maker, rejoices: she determined to enlarge the circumference of her husband's eating habits. Her culinary skill has made him a gourmet — though never a gourmand.

Although the mansion is staffed with seven servants, there is nothing the Greens enjoy more than gathering round the marble-topped table in the kitchen — sometimes inviting close friends to join them — and raiding the refrigerator; or on Springfield's stifling summer evenings having parties in the little garden behind the Mansion, where Mrs. Green had a grill installed.

This installation is part of another cause that would be the joy of any woman, which Mrs. Green embraced on her arrival in Springfield when she determined to restore the hundred-year-old Executive Mansion to its onetime charm and stateliness — to make it an inviting and comfortable home for the family, a mansion worthy of the State of Illinois for official entertaining, and a pleasant and efficient place for the Governor to work in his office on the first floor. She brought to this task exquisite taste, a fine feeling for harmony, and an understanding of the combination of beauty, comfort, and utility.

The war with its shortages stymied her, of course, just as it stymied every housewife in the United States. And as with most other housewives, she engaged in war work — knitting for the Red Cross, serving as a Gray Lady, and working in the blood bank. Nancy also did volunteer work in a Springfield hospital.

Meanwhile, Mrs. Green kept at the job of doing over the Mansion, and she is still at it. Unhappily or happily, according to whether you believe it is more important to build the nest than to teach the young birds to fly, the family rarely is in Springfield to enjoy the home Mrs. Green made for them.

Nancy is at college. Gloria is at preparatory school. The Governor has to be away frequently on official business. When he is in Springfield, about the only time Mrs. Green sees him is at the dinner table. After dinner he goes to his office in the mansion. The clock is more likely to point toward 2:00 or 3:00 A.M. than toward midnight when he emerges.

"It gets mighty lonesome," Mrs. Green recently confided to a friend, "rambling about in that big house without my husband or my children for company." She wasn't complaining, she was stating a fact; long before she talked to her children the day after Dwight Green was elected

Governor she had learned that the price of public service is disruption of family life.

Maybe there was prescience in Gloria's question to her father about the time she was getting ready to celebrate her fifth birthday. Dwight Green had come home from Syracuse, Indiana, where the Miami Indians had made him an honorary chief in their tribe. "Daddy," sobbed his younger daughter, "now that you're an Indian chief, aren't you going to live with us any more?"

The Greens enjoy the friends they have made in Springfield and delight to entertain them, but the Governor's heavy schedule leaves few opportunities for these informal affairs. So aside from these occasions, or when she is attending state events such as the opening of the General Assembly and the annual ten-day State Fair, or being hostess at official luncheons, teas, dinners and parties, Mrs. Green spends much of her time in Chicago.

The Greens have a high rating with newspapermen who watch the passing scene with a cold eye and a chilly appreciation of those who pass. This is not strange in the case of the Governor with his background of newspaper work, but Mrs. Green — whose frankness is not confined to expressing her dislike of spats — won her place in the hearts of reporters and photographers by understanding their problems and helping them to solve them.

In the mayoralty campaign nine years ago photographers came up one early morning to get a layout of pictures of the Greens — Father, Mother, and the children — at home with all the intimate touches that editors demands of photographers, and readers demand in their newspapers.

"Take your coat off, Pete," said one of the photographers

without undue familiarity, for Dwight Green had been "Pete" to Chicago newspapermen around the Federal Building, "and we'll get a swell shot of you at the breakfast table in your shirtsleeves and suspenders." Mrs. Green objected.

"I don't think a picture like that would help him," she said. "My husband   never comes to the table without his coat. We don't live that way and I don't think you should take a picture of him that way."

Dwight Green kept his coat on. But if that photographer had asked Mrs. Green then, or now that she is the first lady of Illinois, to take down the drapes and move six pieces of furniture so he could get a better shot, she would do it. It didn't take the reporters and photographers long to learn that.

This quality of consideration for others and the quality of understanding the things that go on in human hearts and minds, are shared by Dwight and Mabel Green. They are exacting people but far more exacting of themselves than of others.

There is a little group of men who by the nature of their governmental duties are closely associated with the Governor. There is not one among them but who, as the saying goes, would cut off his right arm for the Chief. And there is not one among them who does not know in his heart that the Chief would go the limit for him.

This little group is composed of men who, like the Governor, know how to work and like to work. This group finds fun in those long sessions at the mansion that cut deeply into the hours before daybreak — the fun that men derive from accomplishment.

Along about 2:00 or 3:00 A.M., sometimes later, whenever the body and mind flash the signals of fatigue that preclude good work, the governor orders bacon and eggs, and toast and coffee, each to his own liking — the eggs soft or well basted, sunny side up or over, the bacon crisp or soft. This is served at the long conference table. And there these men have the recompense of good food, good comradeship, and good faith in each other.

Dwight and Mabel Green have tried to imbue their children with this way of life. The record indicates that they have succeeded.

Away back, as time goes in a child's life, when they were students in the grade classes of Miss Harris' school in Chicago, the children won gadgets for proficiency in their studies. Even under the high educational standards established by their parents and demanded by their teachers, Nancy and Gloria had time to learn to become good swimmers and good horsewomen, and to care for pets that included, at various times in Chicago and Springfield, dogs, cats, birds, white mice, tropical fish, turtles, ducks, a pig which Gloria named Confucius, chickens, and two rabbits — that is, there were only two when the children first got them.

And although Duke, the seven-year-old Doberman Pinscher at the Mansion is the Governor's dog, of course Nancy and Gloria made Duke their pet, too. Duke has been ailing recently. If anything should happen to Duke, Dwight Green is quickly going to find himself with a new dog, his favorite breed, an Irish Setter. Mrs. Green has her plans all made.

The white mice, the tropical fish, Confucius, and all the

rabbits are gone from the Mansion now. So are the children. So Dwight and Mabel Green, as with all parents, live with their memories.

They remember the girls' slumber parties in the Mission when every bed and every couch was occupied and girls were bedded down even on the floor, and Mother had the job of feeding them. They remember when Father would climb aboard the sidewalk snowplow that is kept at the Mansion and clean every sidewalk in the block, the kids riding along and shrieking until they got back home, when Daddy would get out the sleds and go belly sliding with them on the hills.

They remember the time that Gloria, then about eleven years of age, upon seeing a Palomino at a horse show, exclaimed, "Daddy, Mommie, that's what I'd like." A friend of the family near by heard the child and sent one down from Chicago in a horse truck. When Gloria came in from a Saturday afternoon's play and was taken out to the garage, temporarily converted to stable use, her eyes were far wider than they were the day after Daddy was elected Governor, but her voice was less audible. Almost prayerfully she murmured, "Is it really mine?"

They remember the strep infection which struck Nancy when she was little more than a baby and left her with a heart murmur which appeared intermittently thereafter. And Mrs. Green, especially, remembers the day a dozen years later when, after Nancy had been given a physical examination, the doctor told her that the heart murmur was apparent again.

Not long after Nancy came home from her Springfield high school, her eyes reflecting her joy, to announce that she had been elected captain of her basketball team. Once again Mrs. Green had to take her daughter in her arms. Quietly she listened to the bitterly disappointing news that she could not captain the team, that she could not even play. The manner in which she took the news was a tribute to the judgment of the teammates who elected her.

The Greens remember Christmas Eves, some white, some green, but all beautiful and all purely family affairs, with a tree in the bay window of the Mansion living room and another in the bay window of the music room so it appeared that they reflected one another; and Christmas morning when breakfast was always first and the children almost choked in excitement until the meal would be over and Daddy would play Santa Claus.

They remember the Easter Parade, with the children in their new finery, after the family had attended services at Springfield's Christ Episcopal Church, of which the Governor is vestryman.

They remember Nancy's first big party when she was sixteen and Gloria's when she was fifteen. But the best remembrance they have, maybe because it is so near and maybe because it was such fun, is of the vacation they all had together during the summer of 1947. The Greens are unanimous that it was the best vacation they ever had.

They hid out up near Hayward, Wisconsin. They wore blue jeans and they roughed it. The governor loves to fish, and he fished to his heart's content.

Mrs. Green went fishing, too. She had practiced back home with a rod and reel guaranteed not to backlash which were given to the Governor. Mrs. Green found them and decided to try them out in the yard at the Mansion. She thought she was doing pretty well until she looked up and discovered she had a considerable gallery on the sidewalk. It didn't take her long to put that rod and reel back with the Governor's things. "I felt like a fool," she said.

Up there at Hayward, Gloria, who had broken eighteen out of twenty-five the third time she ever shot, beat Daddy at skeet shooting. Up there everybody was physically tired and mentally relaxed by bedtime, and bedtime comes early in that country. The Governor took his detective stories to bed with him, but he didn't finish them as he does in bed at home. Sleep always won the race to the last page.

The "best vacation we ever had" over, Gloria packed her bags and went off to Emma Willard School at Troy, New York; Nancy packed hers and went off to a term at the Sorbonne in Paris. She is still regularly enrolled as a student at Smith College.

Nancy went over tourist class. She advised her mother that although she'd like to go on a faster ship the next time, she doesn't want to go first class. "They don't know how to have fun the way tourist class does," she wrote.

27

THE PEOPLE'S MONEY

IT IS IMPOSSIBLE TO SET DOWN AN INTELLIGIBLE chronological history of a state administration. Any attempt to do so must read like — for it would be — the condensed diary of a man trying to do too many things. Such is the Governor's job.

Therefore the historian must take up one phase of state activity at a time, and pursue the record of that phase through official documents, press clippings, and the memory of the men who participated in that phase, until he has pieced together a connected story of that activity, and then return to the beginning to take up another. For no better reason than it has always seemed of first importance to Dwight Green, we now undertake the chronicle of his seven-year war to keep Illinois financially sound.

As has been seen, his declaration of principles in his inaugural message placed honesty in government first, and efficiency and economy second. Such expressions are normal — one might say platitudinous — in any inaugural speech; they are to be found in almost every party platform and certainly in every Republican platform. But the people of Illinois — including the Republicans — were to find that Dwight Green intended to live by them. The lessons in individual thought which had been imbedded in him by his father, uncles, and grandfather in Ligonier had become the only workable economic philosophy which he could understand, and he applied it to governments as well as to individuals.

In his first legislative session, the stark necessity of an empty treasury had supported his recommendations for reduced expenditures and the maintenance of a balanced budget. Even so, he had proceeded with the reduction of the retailers' occupational tax from three to two cents. When the Sixty-third General Assembly convened in 1943, the partisan joy which had prevailed at the inaugural two years before had been replaced by the gloom occasioned by the reverses America had suffered in the first year of World War II. But the State Treasury was in much better shape. The frugal management of the Green administration was bearing fruit, and these savings had been augmented by high revenues during the short prewar prosperity and employment gains of 1941.

Revenues had declined somewhat in 1942, and the experts who had been assembled by Director of Finance McKibbin to make the most thorough study of state finances which had ever been attempted in Illinois, saw no reason to expect much change in the situation in the next two years. Therefore, the Governor urged the Assembly to reduce appropriations further, even in the face of rising costs incidental to the war. He urged most strongly that the State live within its income in those two years, and that the cash balances previously accumulated be preserved to meet postwar needs.

In the Governor's budget message of April 21, 1943, he proclaimed what was to become a cardinal principle of the Green fiscal policy in these words:

"The urgent recommendation is that the reserve be kept intact to meet the demands of the postwar period — the rehabilitation of returning soldiers, replacement and improvement of obsolescent public works, and other capital outlay. The retention of this reserve will do much to avoid an increase in state taxes, or the creation of a heavy public debt in postwar years."

The legislature, sobered by the grim war headlines, followed the Governor's economy program. The budget total was decreased despite increases in the appropriations for the public schools, for special defense activities, and for the establishment of a state system of aid to dependent children. Throughout the remainder of the first term as Governor, the Green administration hewed to the line of its economy program while the Treasury balances continued to swell as the higher prices and increased spending of wartime raised the dollar volume of taxable business in Illinois. The economy record of the Green administration became a pointed argument in the campaign of 1944 when the Governor was re-elected — although the State once more was carried by the New Deal President, up for his fourth term.

The situation was radically changed, however, when the Sixty-fourth General Assembly met in 1945. In the first place, the grim pessimism over the war which prevailed in 1943 had given place to optimism for final victory and all sorts of grandiose schemes for postwar private and public spending. In the second place, many practical Republicans, observing the narrow margin by which their party had retained control of the State administration, were impressed with the political folly of a policy of frugality which had accumulated more than a hundred million dollars and which, by a slight change in the vote percentages, would have been available to a Democratic administration for spending. In the third place, the emphasis on the accumulated reserve in the campaign had encouraged all who benefited from any state expenditures to feel they could expect much larger appropriations in the next session. Moreover, local governments whose financial condition was much less favorable than the State's, and which had been taught by the New Deal to expect large contributions from Federal sources — which had been curtailed by the war expenditures — began to demand much assistance from the State Government.

Finally, the people of Illinois were beginning to talk about a bonus which would be paid after victory to the fighting men of the State, and the suggestion was raised in many quarters that the funds for the bonus could be provided from the reserves in the State Treasury. Against all these demands it was evident that it would take convincing logic, forcefully presented, to keep the Assembly behind the conservative program of living within its income and utilizing its reserves for those capital improvements to which it had been committed.

Governor Green supplied that logic. In his second inaugural message he informed the Assembly that he proposed to submit two separate budgets to the legislature, the first to be the regular operating budget providing for the ordinary functions of the State Government from the revenues to be collected in the next biennium; the second a postwar capital improvement budget covering a program of needed state improvements recommended by the Illinois Postwar Planning Commission — to be financed from the accumulated reserve in the Treasury.

Eventually that program was adhered to, although with the Republican majority in the House reduced by the 1944 election (and with the Republican membership further cut by death and illness until later in the session it was impossible to muster the 77 Republicans necessary for a constitutional majority to pass a bill), the Governor's position could only be maintained by arguments sound enough to convince independent Democrats to vote with him.

One of the most convincing of these arguments was the constructive character of the improvements proposed to be built with the Treasury Reserve funds. To the University of Illinois and the five State colleges went the lion's share of the 139 millions of dollars appropriated in Senate Bill 417, in which all the recommendations of the Postwar Planning Commission were assembled. Provision was made for extensive new buildings on campuses where all building operations had been suspended during the depression and where the authorities were preparing for the rush of students which was sure to come after the war.

cessity for increased teacher salaries, looked to the State funds for the money to provide them. Although the State's contributions for school purposes had been substantially increased by each General Assembly in the Green administration and the total had risen from 29 millions in 1939 to 55 millions in 1945 — an all-time high — proposals were now championed by educational organizations which would have required at least one hundred million dollars for the next biennium. And almost every legislator had his own pet project for which he wanted a million dollars or two for his own community.

It was obvious that Governor Green was in for the legislative battle of his life if he was to sustain the principles of State financing which he had espoused. No one knew that better than Green. The keynote of the address he delivered at the opening session of the Legislature was, "Economy must be our watchword." He reviewed the progress of the capitol improvement plan and said it must be re-examined in the light of current needs and costs. He insisted that there be no increase in State taxes and that the State should continue to live within its current income.

His message which submitted the budget to the Assembly in April put the facts coldly before the legislature. "We are dealing in this budget with inflationary dollars and, as a consequence, it is the largest in our history."

The total for the operating budget was 822 millions of dollars for the two-year period. It provided large increases for the operation of the State's University and colleges, and for the maintenance of the State Welfare institutions. It pointed out the fact that 73.5 per cent of each State dollar was going for relief and education. It recommended appropriations totaling 69 million dollars for the common school fund and other State contributions for special school services — an increase of approximately 14 millions. He met bluntly the challenge of those who were demanding a much larger increase in the school appropriation, saying, "I am also aware that there are bills now pending before the Honorable Bodies which require a State school contribution far in excess of the figures in this budget. Those measures are among those I had in mind when I stated that there are many laudable plans for extension of State activities that our pocketbook will not now permit."

He cited the facts in U. S. Census figures that the citizens of Illinois were paying an average of only $41 per person in State taxes as compared with $70 in California, $67 in New York, and a national average of $45. He pointed out that Illinois levied no State property tax and no State income tax and pledged himself against increases in taxation. He trimmed to the bone the capitol improvement program, but insisted that the buildings most urgently needed for the educational institutions and the Welfare institutions must be completed. He warned that if these necessary improvements were not paid for with the accumulated cash balances in the Treasury, they would have to be paid for by increased State taxes or increased State debt.

Veterans of the press gallery privately admitted that the Governor's logic was very sound, but predicted that it could not stand up against the school lobby or the demands of the municipalities. For a time it looked as if they were right. A school appropriation bill, sponsored by the school authorities and appropriating almost twice as much as the Governor had recommended, passed the House with only three dissenting votes. Yet as the legislators grappled with the problem which the Governor had laid before them — that theirs was the task to distribute the State funds as they saw fit, but that he would insist upon preserving a balanced budget for Illinois — they began to rally to the Governor's program. The battle did not end until past midnight on the last day of the session. The final solution was a compromise in which approximately 10 million dollars more were provided for the common school fund, but the budget remained balanced and the additions were effected by reductions elsewhere. Illinois remained sound.

Throughout the session, the Governor was keenly aware of the genuine financial plight of many of the municipalities of the State; although, as he told a group of Chicago businessmen who had been invited by the Mayor to consider that city's financial problems, he did not believe in improving the insolvency of one branch of the government by destroying the solvency of another. He urged the municipalities to offer suggestions for legislative action which would permit them to raise additional revenues. Both the Chicago and downstate city officials were loath to recommend new city taxes to meet their needs. Finally, on its own initiative, the General Assembly passed, and the Governor signed, a law which permits cities or counties to levy, after a referendum vote, a local retailers' occupational tax of one-half cent on the dollar to be collected for them by the machinery of the State Revenue Department.

The inflationary spiral did not die with the adjournment of the legislature, and the problem of the cities became more acute. So far, no municipality has availed itself of the remedy provided by the legislature, although the clamor for State largess continues. The Governor of Illinois clings to his midwestern convictions that men and cities and states can be really free only when they pay their own way.

— 28 —

WAR JOB

DWIGHT GREEN HAD BEEN GOVERNOR OF ILLINOIS for eleven months lacking six days when the news from Pearl Harbor shocked every American. As he hurried to his desk that Sunday afternoon of December 7, 1941, his thoughts, like those of many physically fit men who had served their country in the First World War, instinctively turned to service on the battle front. He was thirty-three days from his forty-fifth birthday, and the rugged constitution he had built up in his athletic days was still his. But he also was the Governor of nearly eight million people in the nation's third largest state, in the heart of the industrial and agricultural Midwest. The enormity of the problems confronting the wartime Governor of Illinois and the vast opportunity for service in quickly and efficiently mobilizing the State's resources for war inevitably pointed to the dismissal of personal preference.

The citizens of Illinois were no more mentally prepared for Pearl Harbor than the rest of the nation, but the State was not entirely unprepared physically for the shock of war. For eleven months the Governor had increasingly devoted the State's governmental resources and the influence of his office to accelerating the defense effort on the farm and in the factory and wherever the security of the State and Nation might be increased. And as the portents of war cast their ominous shadows across the citizens who worked and prayed for peace, the State administration built the foundation that was to keep Illinois first among the states in many phases of the war effort on the home front. Victory gardens, first planted in Illinois in the spring of 1941 as thrift gardens, salvage drives, plant protection, civil protection, and many aspects of what came to be known as civilian defense were familiar to the citizens of the State by the time of Pearl Harbor.

The first thing Dwight Green did when he got to his desk that Sunday afternoon was to send a telegram to the President pledging the man power, the dollars, and the products of Illinois to unlimited use and co-operation in winning the war. The next thing he did was to call in his fellow State officers and his Cabinet and other principal advisers and to begin work on a program that would make the pledge effective.

Partisan politics were out, he said; the war would not be fought by Democrats or Republicans but by Americans, and the war would not be won by those who fought on the battle fronts unless every person on the home front made the war his chief, if not his only concern. For this reason he decided to make the State Council

of Defense, a nonpartisan agency created by the General
Assembly, the powerhouse for Illinois' war machine.

At once, the Governor summoned a special session of
the legislature — the first wartime emergency special session called in any state in the Union — and asked for the
money and measures to put Illinois out in front in the
war effort and to keep her there.

The General Assembly agreed to Governor Green's
request that it authorize doubling the size of the Illinois
Reserve Militia to 10,000 officers and men. The Reserve
Militia had been organized to take over the job of preserving internal security when the Illinois Guard was
called into Federal service in March, 1941. Thus it was
that two days after Pearl Harbor Illinois had militiamen
on guard at every vital area in the State.

Those were the days when men were beginning to
treasure their tires as highly as they treasured their whole
automobile. The legislature made it a one-to-ten-year
prison offense to steal automobile tires. It concurred in the
Governor's suggestion to give the State Department of
Public Health authority to establish health zones, and
the means of maintaining health in co-operation with
local governments, in areas around military camps and war
production facilities, many of which were situated in un-
incorporated parts of the counties.

The legislators also made three-quarters of a million
dollars available to the Defense Council, which had been
operating under a $50,000 appropriation. The use of the
larger appropriation was a striking example of the Green
method of economy without stinting the job. After organizing and putting into high gear a state-wide Citizens'

Defense Corps and a Citizens' Service Corps, which fulfilled the Governor's orders to put Illinois out in front in the war effort and keep her there, the Defense Council, some two years later, turned back to the State's general fund a few dollars less than a quarter million dollars of its appropriation. Subsequent appropriations were smaller, and the amounts unexpended were larger percentagewise.

The Defense Council, the name of which was changed later to Illinois War Council, had as members certain state officers and representatives of the Republican majority and the Democratic minority in the General Assembly, who were designated by law, and private citizens who were appointed by the Governor as chairman of the Council.

To fill these places and others on special committees created by the Council, Governor Green enlisted highly regarded and well-known leaders in industry, labor, education, business, agriculture, medicine, publishing, the law, the ministry, veterans' affairs, and women's activities. He prevailed on the late Frank O. Lowden, Illinois' great World War I Governor, to serve as honorary chairman and to counsel and advise the group. He then appointed the late Major General Frank Parker, a distinguished soldier who had commanded the First Division, A.E.F., in World War I, executive director of the Council.

The make-up of the War Council is significant because it is typical of the Green approach to the problem which confronted him. It was a problem which required for solution that men and women of special talents be given specific jobs and the authority and responsibility they needed to carry out their assignments. It also is significant because the leadership which Illinois consistently maintained in the war effort was due in large degree to the kind of men and women on whom the Governor prevailed to give freely of their time and experience and energy in the work of the Council.

Here was a group dedicated to the single purpose of seeing that Illinois did everything humanly possible to assist in winning the war. When they came from every section of the state for their regularly scheduled meetings, the Negro minister from Chicago's South Side and the great industrialist from central Illinois would compare notes; the matron who spoke for 700,000 Illinois clubwomen and the president of the State Federation of Labor would exchange ideas; the Republican editor of two downstate newspapers and the Democratic legislator from Chicago's teeming West Side would discuss their special problems; the past state commander of the American Legion and the farmer from southern Illinois would pass along suggestions.

Out of this pool of ideas, opinions, suggestions, and plans that represented the thinking and manner of living of all the State's citizens, came the programs that were the starting points of many of Illinois' war efforts. From those points the people of Illinois went on to plant more victory gardens than any state in the Union in each of the war years; to consistent leadership in the salvage of metals and paper; to one of the four National Security Awards that were the first made, simultaneously, by the Office of Civilian Defense for industrial plant protection and security, and to many other firsts in the battle on the home front.

Just as important as the fact that Illinois planted more

Nancy Green enthusiastically kisses Daddy, as Governor Green is called by his daughters, while younger daughter Gloria gives hearty buss to her mother. Forthcoming visit of Santa Claus is discussed by the Governor and his young friend at annual Christmas party for children in Springfield.

The first anniversary of Pearl Harbor finds Governor Green taking inventory of Illinois' wartime accomplishments and obligations at a meeting of the State Defense Council.

than 600,000 victory gardens in the first year of the war, and more than a million the second year, was the impact of this successful program on the nation. After the first year's success, officials of the U. S. Department of Agriculture, the National Victory Gardens Institute, and representatives of many states came to Illinois to proclaim the State's program the outstanding one in the nation and to adopt the pattern for national and state use.

And just as important as the millions of pounds of metals and paper and fats and greases that were salvaged in Illinois were the patterns for these salvage drives that were first used in the State. For these patterns were adopted nationally and channeled into other states by the salvage division of the War Production Board.

While Governor Green was using the facilities of State Government to make these wartime activities successful, and was urging his fellow citizens to participate in them, he practiced what he preached. He and Mrs. Green and their children, Nancy and Gloria, organized their own salvage drive in the neighborhood of the Executive Mansion. It netted a ton and a half of scrap metal and half a ton of newspapers and magazines. A junk dealer paid $21.60 for the stuff. The money was used to buy smokes for the Yanks.

When rationing officials were overwhelmed by the job of packaging and sending out the first sugar ration books — and distributing them to consumers — a telephone call to the War Council's women's division solved the problem. Twenty-four hours later as many of the 700,000 women as were needed to do the job were at their posts of duty in cities, towns, and villages throughout the State.

State drew when Federal rationing made it impossible to obtain normal replacements of worn-out cars used in essential services.

It was not long before the yearly mileage of State cars was cut in half.

Governor Green preached and practiced the economy of conservation, and he preached and practiced the economy of saving. His official practice of the economy of saving enabled the State Government to invest something like $40,000,000 in government bonds up to the time he bought a pig for a million dollars.

It was a navy pig named King Neptune. The day the Governor bought King Neptune it was Franklin County's victory pig; it had already brought more than $1,000,000 when it was placed on the auction block at West Frankfort.

"I'll bid a million," the Governor said. Nobody gasped. Nobody was astonished. The auctioneer said "Sold," and State Treasurer William G. Stratton handed him a check for $1,000,000.

Somebody had already bought the squeal of the pig, somebody else had bought the tracks it made in the mud. And everybody had waived his right to what he had purchased, and took war bonds instead.

Governor and Mrs. Green also practiced the economy of conservation — to increase the amount of essential foodstuffs for military use — and the economy of saving — to increase their personal war bond purchases — in the Executive Mansion. The practice was in the serving of substitute foods and the preparation of inexpensive meals.

Soybean loaf was one of the conservation-economy dishes served at the Mansion — a pound of beef, three ounces of salt pork, a quarter pound of soybean grits, four ounces of bread crumbs, and a few other ingredients. You could throw that together and serve six people. And you could save those precious ration points for occasions when, as governor, you entertained Viscount Halifax, British Ambassador to the United States, and Lady Halifax, at dinner during a wartime tour which took them to the Executive Mansion.

And so the days went, and most of the nights, too, in conferences, meetings, discussions, necessary trips of inspection, and the performance of the thousand and one duties and obligations that fell upon the shoulders of this quiet, smiling, determined Governor whose hair was rapidly whitening. He never was too busy to listen to and try to help solve the other fellow's problem. And he made clear by his actions, his attitudes, and his words that he understood that "things don't just happen." When he handed out a tough assignment, and got a creditable job on time, he knew and made it clear to his associates and subordinates that he knew the thought and toil and the tedious follow-up of detail which they had put into their accomplishments.

"Things didn't just happen" in the Governor's office. They were planned, and worked at, and followed through. And so he knew that "it didn't just happen" that those to whom he delegated responsibility for carrying out the coal conservation program were successful; that in the face of wartime shortages of men and materials, his highway officials kept open and in repair the State's great network of highways, over which were hauled millions of pounds of essential war material; and that the men to whom he handed his plan for bus service for workers in war plants not accessible by other forms of public transportation, turned those plans into buses running on schedule.

Every problem was approached with one consideration: Will it help the war effort? For many years Illinois has been famous for its great State Fair; considerably more than a million people attended it last year. But when the Army indicated it could use the vast fairgrounds, there was no hesitation.

"The Army says it needs the fairgrounds for its air force," the Governor told his State Fair Board. "If the Army needs it, we should turn it over. Besides, it takes tires and railroad equipment to get to the fair. And our people who would attend it will devote those ten days to producing the food and implements needed for war."

And so it was that Illinois gave up her greatly cherished State Fair for four years. And so it was, on the basis of the one consideration of helping the war effort, that the Governor agreed to attend a series of thirty-four war rallies and WAC recruitment campaign meetings in thirty-one cities. It was a back-breaking schedule that kept him on the road for most of forty-five days of miserable November and December weather. He carried part of his other work with him and would hurry back to Springfield whenever possible to attend to the rest of it there. But the WAC campaign was successful, and the war rallies resulted in more salvage, more bond purchases, more production, more conservation, and more wartime activities in general.

While Dwight Green worked strenuously at these problems of government and civilian welfare that were brought on by the war, he spent long hours in thought and conference on two vital postwar problems. One was the problem of rehabilitating and expanding the State's educational, welfare, and service institutions, its mental and other hospitals, the other of improving and expanding transportation — railroads, highways, airports, and waterways — throughout the State, with special emphasis on the Chicago metropolitan area. Emphasis was placed on Chicago because for a decade a complacent local government had made itself conspicuous by lack of accomplishments in public works.

Shortages of men and material had made it an heroic job even to keep State institutions properly repaired, much less to enlarge them. And the Governor early in the war foresaw that the State's university and teachers' colleges, its hospitals, and especially its mental institutions would be woefully inadequate to care for the postwar bulge which he was certain would come.

Here were the places to put part of that $1,000,000 paid for King Neptune and other monies that were saved to create an eventual State reserve fund of approximately $200,000,000. The larger the reserve grew, the greater grew the pressures to raid it. But those who tried it — and their number was great, their suggestions precious — ran up against the Pete Green of Ligonier, who had saved a few hundred dollars against the day he should go off to school; the Pete Green of Wabash College, who spent his summer vacations hauling lumber for, among other reasons, "the matter of revenue"; the Pete Green who had been reared to the kind of working and living that at each year's end saw a little more accumulated than the year before.

Yes, said Dwight Green, the place for those dollars is in rehabilitating, expanding, and improving the State institutions; in a program of airport expansion and expressways to connect the ports with crowded cities they serve; in a highway and waterway system, and in railroad freight and passenger terminal facilities that would give free circulation to commerce and industry in which there had been near-stagnation.

The General Assembly acquiesced in his suggestion that the legislators create a Postwar Planning Commission. Dwight Green manned this Commission as he had manned the War Council, with experts in business, finance, industry, transportation, education, commerce, engineering, and so on — big men, important men who accepted his invitation to serve for the good of their State and their communities, and a small, skillful staff of paid employees.

He gave them their assignment — "The broad problem of planning for a new era." He told them not to be unduly influenced by prewar prejudices, because "History turned a new leaf when war started. It will turn another leaf when the war is ended."

From the day men began to surge home from the war and materials began to trickle into normal markets, Illinois has reaped dividends from the Governor's initiation of postwar planning. The job is far from finished, of course, but a good start has been made because the State and its citizens knew where they were going when the day came to move, and the dollars were there to keep them going. No, "things don't just happen."

The other problem on which the Governor spent long hours of thought and study and conference was the veterans' problem and the problems that would confront the individual veteran when he came back from the war to try to pick up where he had left off in civil life. That is another chapter, one of the brightest chapters in the history of Illinois, and certainly in the two administrations of Dwight H. Green.

29

AS THE BOYS CAME HOME

ILLINOIS GAVE SOMEWHAT MORE THAN 900,000 OF HER
sons and daughters to the fighting services, just
about one of every eight residents of the state. Long
before most of them had gone off to the camps where they
were trained in the ways of war, Dwight Green had begun
to think of the problems that would confront the veterans
when they returned to their homes, their jobs, their schools.

He remembered the shameful years after War I: lack
of hospitals for the mentally sick and the physically sick
and wounded; lack of a place to care for those suffering
from the nervous disorders bred at war, many of whom
ended up in mental institutions; lack of method to get the
right man into the right job, and all too often lack of any
job; lack of any plan for veterans' rehabilitation and employment; lack of money to do what needed to be done,
and, on the face of it, a lack of interest in what needed to be
done.

Above all, he remembered "the old run-around." He once put it this way in a talk to Illinois veterans' service officers: ". . . we have eliminated shuffling the veteran from one agency to another while he desperately searches for the one concerned with his particular need. That, gentlemen, is what you and I, when we came home from the war twenty-five years ago, called the old run-around. And that, gentlemen, is out — definitely out — in Illinois now."

But that talk was made something more than three and a half years after the thought and study and conferences in which were developed Illinois' program for human reconversion from war to peace and for the rehabilitation and employment of veterans whose disabilities deprived them of the normal means of earning a living. The mainspring of the movement was to help Illinois veterans to help themselves.

The Governor early made it clear that he did not care how the veteran was helped or who helped him — the Federal Government, the State, the communities, or private groups — but that he must be helped if he needed help. Leaping ahead again momentarily, we find him saying after the Congress had enacted the so-called G. I. Bill of Rights:

"Our own State of Illinois has made available scores of benefits and services for our veterans. No matter what the Federal Government has prepared to do for the veteran, no matter what public and private organizations have arranged, in the last analysis, here in Illinois, we regard our own veterans as our own responsibility. The Illinois veteran who finds other doors closed to him can come to the door of his own State and he will find it open for him. The Illinois veteran who has help coming to him from other sources, but who is in distress while awaiting that help, can seek help from his own State, and he will get it."

This was the kind of thinking that guided the planning which had as its first concrete result the Governor's Committee on Veterans' Rehabilitation and Employment. In his executive order of February 9, 1943, creating the Committee, the governor wrote, "The State can never discharge in full its obligation to the veterans, but it can, by proper administration of a co-ordinated program of rehabilitation, repay in part a most urgent debt of honor."

The date of the signing was fourteen months and two days after Pearl Harbor; the war in Europe still had more than two years to run, in the Pacific two and one-half years. But Illinois already had the blueprints of a comprehensive veterans' service program. The next job was for the Governor's Committee to do the groundwork and lay the foundation.

The membership of this Committee once again gives evidence of the Green approach to a problem of great magnitude: get the best men available for the job and give them authority commensurate with their responsibility. To the chairmanship of the Committee the governor called a World War I veteran, James P. Ringley, a businessman who was a past state commander of the American Legion, and who for twenty-five years had devoted all his spare time to veterans' service. He was equally at home with business and political leaders, and with the officers and rank and file of veterans' organizations, and he had the confidence and respect of all.

A highly placed industrialist, Harvey E. Ellerd, vice-president of Armour and Co., accepted the governor's invitation to head the Advisory Committee on Employment; a specialist in industrial medicine, Dr. H. A. Vonachen, winner of the Knudsen award for his contributions in that field, took the chairmanship of the Advisory Committee on Industrial Medicine; State officers and members of the Cabinet who headed offices and departments — such as Public Instruction, Public Health, Labor, Agriculture — with services that the veterans would need, were named. As administrator the Governor appointed Homer Bradney, a man with organizing ability; he knew how to get along with people and had spent most of the time since he came home from World War I in veterans' service.

The Committee set out to hoe its row, and a tough row it was. None knew better than the man who appointed the Committee that a blueprint for a statewide veterans' service was one thing; translating that blueprint into the dollar, the equipment, and the men to perform that service was another. The Committee organized and improvised, it tried and rejected it, it tried and retained. But it kept hoeing.

There was no time to lose. Already several thousand veterans had returned. By early 1944 there would be 50,000 of them, one of every three with a disability. As a general rule the veterans who came home first, either because of physical disabilities or sickness, or because they couldn't stand the gaff, or could not adjust themselves to life in the services, were those most greatly in need of assistance.

Those were the days before there was a G.I. Bill of Rights; the State was strictly on its own, and the State, through the Governor and his Committee had said, "Illinois meets its responsibility to the veteran *now*." Illinois did meet it.

The Governor's Committee began to function as a central information and referral agency with access to every resource and every service of every department of State Government under jurisdiction of the Governor, and in co-operation with the veterans' organizations and other groups eager to and in a position to serve the veteran.

The case of "John Doe" — and it is an actual case listed in the Committee's files — illustrates the method of operation. "John" came back to Chicago minus his left arm, which he lost while operating a fourteen-inch gun on the U.S.S. "New York." From the newspapers and the radio he learned that the posts of every veterans' organization, and every State Department and Bureau were contact stations for the Committee. It also had 1,100 accredited representatives in every section of the State. One of these sent "John" to Committee headquarters.

The interviewer was a youngish veteran of World War I who had a son in World War II and who had a permanent disability from his service in the A.E.F. He had experience in veterans' service, and he had in his mind the urgent admonition of his Governor:

"Always remember that the veteran who has come to you is an individual with his own individual hopes and fears, sorrows and joys, ambitions and desires, and wants and needs. We are not going to run these human beings who have fought for us through a mill. Human interest in its very best and fullest understanding is what we need in this job."

The interview disclosed that "John" needed training and

a job, that he had a high-school education and an agreeable manner, that he would like to become an accountant and eventually a C.P.A., and that if someone would point out the road to that goal he would confidently tackle the journey. He was directed to the State Division of Rehabilitation.

After he had been fitted with an artificial arm, at no cost to "John," he was given an aptitude test to determine what he was best qualified to do. The test disclosed a high degree of aptitude for what he wanted to do, but of course it would be necessary for him to go back to school for a special course.

So "John" went back to school, again at no cost to him, for the State paid for the course. This still left the problem of money for essentials while he was studying and "John" wasn't looking for charity; he was looking only for the kind of help that would enable him to help himself. The Employment Assistance Division of the State Department of Labor helped him find a part-time job.

By the time he had finished his course, the Placement Department of the Division of Rehabilitation had a good full-time job in the business world lined up for him. "John" still is in that job, doing nicely, gradually advancing. He spends two nights a week in the College of Business Administration of a great university, continuing the studies which lead to a C.P.A. And "John" now is able to pay for his course and insists on doing it.

The case may not be typical but certainly it is not singular. It illustrates what the Governor's Committee was able to accomplish in its early days and how it laid the groundwork for the present statewide system of veterans'

service under Illinois Veterans' Commission. The big brass
of the Army and Navy, officials of the Veterans' Administration and of other states, and the leaders of veterans'
organizations in the states and the nation have said it is by
far the outstanding veterans' service setup in the country.
Illinois veterans, of whom more than 600,000 have been
given service, swear by it — not at it.

Governor Green and his Committee continued to probe
at the problem of the veterans who came home suffering
from nervous disorders, and the ratio of these among the
first homecomers was considerably larger than among the
bulk of Illinois fighters coming home several years later.
These nervous cases were the men who after World War I
returned to their communities as misfits.

Some had the jitters and couldn't stay put. Some were
surly, or morose, or sullen, or vindictive. Some were
revengeful over fancied wrongs. All lacked ability to
readjust themselves to civil life, but they were not cases
for what in those days usually was referred to as the insane
asylum. Yet many of them ended up there as wards of the
State. Others became public nuisances and sometimes public
menaces. All were liabilities to society and useless to themselves.

The Committee, which had scant funds when it began
to operate — remember, it was created by executive order
and without a legislative appropriation — early interested
the race-track operators of the state in the veterans' service
problem. By conducting so-called charity racing days, and
sometimes by outright gifts from the operators, this group
contributed several hundred thousand dollars in the war
years.

The money went to Illinois Veterans' Services, a non-profit corporation, which might be called a wholly owned subsidiary of the Governor's Committee and which could accept and expend such funds. Some of the money went for such special Committee activities as the purchase of sports and entertainment equipment for veterans' facilities in the state, and for emergency financing of veterans who lacked railroad fare from their homes to Springfield or Chicago or some other city where they could obtain special treatment or service.

But the bulk of the money went to lease and take an option to buy a private hospital on Chicago's West Side, and which some two years later was bought by the State Department of Public Welfare out of a legislative appropriation for that and similar institutions. But that was after the experiment by Governor Green and his Committee had proved so successful that it was acclaimed nationally and delegations from other states and from Canada came to inspect it.

When Illinois Veterans' Services took over the building, certain rooms were rearranged, the most essential equipment was installed, a staff of physicians, psychiatrists, and psychologists was selected, operation was placed in the hands of the Chicago Community Clinic of the Department of Public Welfare, and the doors were opened on the Veterans' Rehabilitation Center for the diagnosis and treatment of veterans with nervous disabilities. It was the first institution of its kind to be opened by any state in the nation.

The operating room of the old Washington Boulevard Hospital, with most of its north wall and the slanted portion of its roof made of glass, became the art room. Near-by rooms were converted to wood, metal, plastic, and leather workshops, and radio repair, weaving, and printing shops. Downstairs was a gymnasium with punching bag, medicine ball, and wrestling mats.

There was a library, a music room, a ping pong room, a card, chess, and checkers room, a lounge, a physical therapy room with sun lamps and rubdown tables, a kitchen and dining room, and thirty-eight bedrooms. And there were of course the rooms necessary for the staff to do its work.

The building was dedicated by Governor Green to help solve what Dr. Thomas A. C. Rennie of the National Committee for Mental Hygiene had referred to as "the biggest medical problem facing our Army today, and civilians for years to come, the psychiatric casualties of World War II." The staff was "concerned with the adjustment of the veteran who has found it emotionally difficult to make the transition from military to civilian life."

The Center's program — which included treatment of inpatients and outpatients, all of whom entered and were free to leave of their own volition — was divided into four major divisions: the occupational, the recreational, the physical, and the educational, all integrated by the prescription of the psychiatrist.

Into the Center came the jittery veteran from Bloomington, the surly one from Rockford, the revengeful one from Cairo, the misfits from Waukegan and Quincy and Effingham and Rock Island, as inpatients, and thousands of outpatients who lived in Chicago, each a potential for mental collapse or for good citizenship, usefulness to society, and an enjoyable life. There was no limit to the time they could remain. It cost them nothing. If they could not afford the railroad fare, Illinois Veterans' Services paid it; those who cannot afford it today have it paid by the State.

The verdict was not long in coming. When the Center had been in operation about a year, 83 per cent of the veterans who had been discharged were listed as cured. A follow-up system after they returned to their communities has not altered that figure substantially.

Today the Illinois program includes establishment of half a dozen such centers in the state. And to serve the veteran who is beyond the borderline of treatment in a center, there is a vast expansion program of mental hospitals.

— 30 —

"ALL YOURS, VETERAN"

A S THE NUMBER OF RETURNING VETERANS INCREASED, the work of the Committee increased and so did its need for man power, especially men who had the making of good service officers. Governor Green authorized the Committee to borrow men from the Code departments, which are headed by the members of his Cabinet, many of whom were on the Committee. The men who showed promise were kept; those who didn't were returned to their old jobs. Quickly the skeleton organization took on substance and was vitalized.

By early 1944 the results of Dwight Green's veterans' service program had captured public approval to the extent that business, labor, industry, agriculture, and other groups were eager to enlarge the parts they were taking in the work of human reconversion. To meet these requests and at the same time increase the usefulness of the Committee's service officers, it was decided to hold a school.

"All Yours, Veteran"

The Illinois Service Officers school, first of its kind in the nation, was held at Jacksonville where, in an accelerated six-day course, instruction was given by specialists from the Veterans' Administration, the Red Cross, industry, departments of state government, agriculture, veterans' organizations, medicine and the law, the United States and State employment offices, and education.

More than 500 men and women — lawyers, ministers, doctors, newspapermen, public service employees, school-teachers, labor leaders, industrial personnel directors, and service officers, among others — attended the school. Their first class was at 8 A.M., their last long after dark. They had to pass written examinations before they received diplomas.

But the midnight that Dwight Green drove back to Springfield after handing out those diplomas, he knew that he had his teeth into the core of his problem in human reconversion. By that night, on the basis of what his Committee had accomplished, he had evolved the plan of a veterans' service organization which, after conferences with legislators and representatives of every veterans' organization in Illinois, was to become the Illinois Veterans' Commission with its 140 field offices — at least one in every county — and its one-stop service for the veteran.

And that was the night he ordered preparation of a booklet telling every right and service and benefit to which the Illinois veteran was entitled from the Federal and State governments, from the communities and public and private organizations, and how he should go about obtaining them without unnecessary loss of time or expenditure of effort. The booklet, "It's All Yours, Veteran," eventually was placed in the hands of as many Illinois veterans and veterans-to-be, or in the homes of their families, as could be reached.

The veteran read not only how to go about getting the big benefits and services — education, on-the-job training, claims, medical care, employment, vocational rehabilitation — as easily as possible, but he also read of many important benefits his own state had provided for him. Above all, it was impressed upon him that he was an individual, not a number, and that as a citizen of Illinois who had fought for his country he was *entitled* to everything the State could do to help him solve his problems as he readjusted himself to civil life.

He was offered help that would enable him to help himself.

As the former service man read "It's All Yours, Veteran," he learned that Illinois had made it possible for him to have his discharge recorded by his county recorder, who also would give him a certified copy — without charge. If his license to be a barber, an insurance agent, a plumber, or any of two score occupations licensed by the State and renewed annually, had lapsed while he was in service, he learned how to get it renewed — without charge. He learned about veterans' special scholarships as the University of Illinois and the state colleges, and that any Illinois veteran who could pass the entrance examinations to these institutions was entitled to as much as four years' tuition — without charge.

He learned that his old job, maybe a better one if he was qualified by his military training, was awaiting him if he had been in State service (the State now has some 6,000 veterans in its employ), and that he could get on-the-job training in his State job; that he was a preferred prospect for a job in the State Highway Police force (the State since has created more than 150 new jobs in the force to which only World War II veterans are eligible). And his widow learned that if her husband had died while on active duty, her sixteen- to twenty-two-year-old children were entitled to $150 a year from the State toward their tuition, board, books, or other expenses while they were in school or college.

They didn't learn that Dwight Green's program of veterans' service was responsible for these things. The booklet did not mention that. But that was the way it was; he had planned it that way.

When the General Assembly met in biennial session in January, 1945, the Governor urged the legislators to consider an emergency appropriation (that would make the money immediately available) of nearly eight million dollars to expand the State's hospital facilities for veterans, and proposed establishment of a veterans' affairs agency as a permanent division of State Government.

"The wide program for service to veterans of this war which Illinois already has undertaken and which no doubt will be expanded, will cost money," Governor Green told the General Assembly. "The people will approve strongly the spending of that money if the great task of helping our returning fighters find their proper place in peacetime society is properly performed."

In a few weeks the legislature had made an emergency appropriation of $7,884,000, of which some $900,000 was for establishment of veterans' rehabilitation centers down-

— later eliminated at the Governor's suggestion on the ground that the person of modest means who sought amusement for relaxation already was paying a stiff Federal tax.

But some of the legislators who long had been itching to dip their hands into the State's cash reserve, which the Governor already had earmarked for essential postwar construction and services, wanted to pay part of the bonus out of the cash on hand and leave the rest to be paid somehow in the future. Governor Green said "No," flatly. He was not going to have his postwar development program wrecked, and he was not going to mortgage the future of Illinois.

The bill was passed by the Senate, but a group of Democrats in the House fought bitterly to strike the tax features from the bill. The Governor stood firm and the bill finally passed in the form suggested by him. But after he had signed the Illinois Veterans' Compensation Act of 1946, there remained one more hurdle — a referendum at the November election.

In the campaign that fall, while some Democrats kept silent on the bonus proposition and some gave it only lip service, the Republicans under Dwight Green's leadership campaigned probably more strenuously for the bonus than they did for state, congressional, or county candidates. Daily they pointed out that under the Illinois Constitution, the bonus act required a majority of all votes cast for members of the General Assembly. Many a proposal which had received a majority of the votes cast on it had failed to carry because of that hurdle.

Broad were the smiles at Republican headquarters and

great was the glee in the homes of veterans when the returns began to come in election night. Early it was clear
that the voters had overwhelmingly approved the bonus.

Quickly the Illinois Service Recognition Board, of which
the Governor, the State Treasurer, and the Adjutant General of the Illinois National Guard are members, built
its organization. Governor Green appointed Admiral John
Downes as director and Colonel Chester L. Fordney of
the Marines, deputy director. In something like six months
veterans began to receive their bonus checks, at a rate which
soon reached more than ten thousand a week.

"The people will approve strongly the spending of that
money," Governor Green had said of the veterans' service
setup, "if the great task . . . . is properly performed."

There are four ways to judge "if the great task" that
was set before it has been "properly performed" by the
Illinois Veterans' Commission.

The first yardstick is what Illinois veterans say about
it. There are, of course, the infinitesimal minority of
chronic grumblers, who can be dismissed just so long
as they remain an infinitesimal minority. The vast majority
of the more than 600,000 veterans who have used the
services of the Illinois Veterans' Commission are enthusiastic about it. It is significant that there has not been
public criticism by the press, by the veterans, or by the
veterans' organizations, but there have been resolutions of
praise by the latter.

Another measuring rod is what outsiders have to say
about it. There has been national acclaim for the Illinois
program, the Illinois organization, and the Illinois per-

land clearance commissions to acquire slum areas for private or public housing redevelopment, or for public purposes other than housing.

5. Power for local authorities to sell or lease property, acquired by condemnation, to private enterprise for housing redevelopment.

6. Liberalization of the State Housing Act to encourage organization of limited dividend corporations to build and operate housing developments.

7. Authorization for Illinois and out-of-state insurance companies to invest in bonds and securities of agencies and corporations engaged in housing or to engage in housing development directly.

The master tool to be furnished by the new legislation was the appropriation of the ten million dollars with which the State Housing Board was to be authorized to make grants to local housing authorities and land-clearance commissions upon approval of their applications for assistance. It was proposed that these grants be made in amounts not exceeding the pro rata share of the total appropriation based on the ratio which the population of an area of operation would bear with respect to the population of the State as a whole. On this basis the Chicago area comprising, roughly, six-eighths of the entire state population, would receive that proportion of the ten millions.

Three of the four housing bills passed, but the fourth — the master tool, a housing grant for ten millions — was shelved. The legislators were of the opinion that the communities should help themselves; they were also of the opinion that a housing program was not nearly so dire a need as Governor Green — who was definitely making

Governor Green sparks a war-bond and WAC-recruiting rally. His organizing ability gave Illinois consistent leadership in wartime activities. The Governor, State Treasurer Rowe (left), and National Guard Adjutant General Boyle, members of Service Recognition Board, discuss the bond issue which gave Illinois World War II veterans the most liberal bonus in the nation.

Governor Green arrives in a helicopter for dedication of Springfield airport. There are few hours during the annual Illinois State Fair when the Governor is not on the fairgrounds. Here he joins a crowd of interested observers as exhibitors show the grand champion barrow of the 1946 Fair.

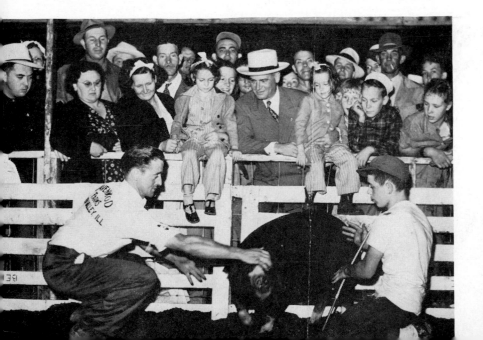

the matter a personal issue — considered it to be; there seemed to be room for everybody, in the opinion of the legislators. It appeared almost as though they had forgotten that several million Americans were absent from the country straightening out a little argument as to whether the world was to be run by a small clique of ruthless bullies or by the choice of the common people through free elections. The housing grant bill had been laid aside — laid aside by men whose eyes had yet to be opened to the fact that while hundreds of thousands would die on the battlefields or as the result of wounds and sickness, there would be millions coming home entitled to places to live, in which to bring up families and to renew the normal life of decent citizens of a nation at peace — at peace largely through their efforts.

Governor Green had eyes for all that. No chief executive of a state ever set out to lobby for a measure as determinedly and as persistently as Dwight Green did. He went among the legislators to convince them of right and justice, of the fearful need of preparedness for what was coming, — a nationwide housing shortage to be unparalleled in the country's history.

He could not go into cloakrooms; he could not buttonhole senators and assemblymen on the street or in hotel lobbies. But he followed a better method. By small groups he invited to the Executive Mansion the members of the legislature. He sat down to dinner with these men night after night — each night a different group. During the meal the subject of housing was taboo; after all, it was proper for the host to direct the trend of conversation. In the agreeable mood that always follows a well-served

[281]

and well-cooked meal the governor encouraged his guests into open conversation; while his several audiences in turn smoked his cigars and sipped their drinks, he fought his battle for houses. These after-dinner sessions at the Mansion ran, always, far into the night; more than once, dawn was breaking as the Governor sought his bed, exhausted by argument. The next night he was at it again with a new group of so-far unconvinced legislators. But he felt he was making headway; the whole business was so absolutely right he knew he could not fail; he knew also that in so far as his duty to those absent soldiers of Illinois was concerned, he must not fail.

He put it over; the bills were resurrected, became law. Among the very first to make application for its pro rata portion of the ten millions was the city of Chicago. But most of those millions which came to Chicago from the State still lie in the banks; the Democratic administration did not want to give a Republican Governor the credit due. In exchange for the millions received by Chicago from the State Housing Board a token effort was made by the city to take options on parcels of land, but few purchases were made. It was the philosophy of the New Deal Kelly administration that clearance of deteriorated areas was a one hundred per cent Federal governmental operation — that private enterprise could do very little in ridding Chicago of its slums. Under the new Illinois housing acts this fallacy of thought was subdued. Private enterprise and local government were to work hand in hand in the redevelopment of distressed construction areas.

According to the bills creating new powers for Housing Authorities and Land Clearance Commissions, the latter became a new municipal agency with the same areas of operation, powers, and duties; it is subject to the same State supervision as Housing Authorities except that the Land Clearance Commission has no authority to build or operate housing.

The response to the passage of the Green-engineered bills throughout the state was tremendous. Twenty-five Housing Authorities blossomed out into 120 as soon as the new legislation came to be understandable. Ninety-seven of the one hundred and two counties took advantage of the act; every city except Elgin came in. The money was available almost coincident with victory on both major fronts. The soldiers were coming home — and there was so little time! But Illinois, thanks to the Governor's habit of looking ahead, was also ahead of every other state in the Union on the matter of a housing program.

Late in 1945 Governor Green decided to call on the Army and Navy to help alleviate the state housing shortage — a shortage which was getting more acute with the discharge of each individual soldier or sailor. The State Housing Board was instructed to open negotiations for the conversion of empty military and naval barracks into veterans' apartments.

"If the Army and Navy approve these conversion plans," said the Governor, "Illinois will participate in the most satisfactory temporary veterans' housing program in the nation."

Approval came in short time for conversion of the barracks at Great Lakes Naval Training Station and Camp Grant. The Housing Board obtained permission to convert veteran apartments at Glenview Naval Air Station.

This program alone has given the State several hundred temporary veteran apartments, a large proportion of which were converted at Great Lakes.

Now, $10,000,000 spread over the municipalities of Illinois, does not give the impression of being any too much money with which to overcome a shortage of thousands of homes — to make land purchase on which to develop homes and to plan for slum clearance and re-development. In truth, by itself, it is not. But as a pump primer for the Governor's broad housing plan, it served its purpose. An example or two of procedure will not be out of place.

The Christian County Housing Authority received a $48,000 state housing grant and turned it into a permanent $300,000 single family veteran housing development in Taylorville, the county seat.

During the war 400 homes had been erected by the Federal Government in the Herrin-Marion area of Williamson County to house a segment of the war workers at the near-by ordnance plant. The Federal Government wanted to liquidate these homes. The Williamson County Housing Authority obtained a $65,116 state housing grant as a basis for the venture, contracted its assets to local, private, nonprofit housing corporations to obtain maximum mortgage insurance on bank loans. The houses were sold on long-term payments to 200 homeseekers in Herrin and to 200 others in Marion.

Soon after the completion of a state-aided temporary 300-trailer housing project, Peoria began to seek ways to turn the 27-acre site into a permanent development. A policy adopted by the State Housing Board demanded that property purchases made with State grants be pressed into immediate use for quick stopgap housing and then be developed as soon as possible into permanent dwellings.

Peoria, complying with this agreement, chose the newly devised community-state plan, which was drafted by the State Housing Board especially for this type of operation. Without any lost motion, the second largest Illinois city went to work. An unoccupied section of the acreage is being improved with water and sewer lines along with sidewalks and streets.

Upon completion, the improved site will be made available to private enterprise, with the Peoria Housing Authority accepting a second mortgage in exchange for the improved ground. If there are no acceptable "takers" within a given period, a private nonprofit corporation will be organized in Peoria — taking the property for development on a second mortgage.

Under this plan of operation, the housing grant funds cannot be construed as a subsidy, but merely as an "opportunity fund" to help private builders meet the rental housing needs of the State.

(Early in the Governor's fight for housing, the State Housing Board drafted a community-state plan to produce rental houses. In operation, this permits the local Housing Authority to use a portion of its State housing grant to purchase a piece of raw land and improve it with streets, sidewalks, and underground needs. Construction loans are obtained from the local banker. FHA underwrites these loans to a maximum of ninety per cent of the assets, and contracts are submitted to begin construction. Under this program any Housing Authority in the State which places $50,000 of State grant funds into a site and its improvements may provide the community with roughly $450,000 worth of housing.)

Yet another angle of the housing program as inaugurated by Governor Green is that of the small home purchase on long- or short-time payments. It must be remembered that 64 per cent of the housing grants were for $25,000 or less. A great segment of the Housing Authorities who fall into this bracket prefer to rotate their funds quickly. An example of this type of development is in Casey, Clark County. The grant is being used to build individual homes for immediate sale. The proceeds of the sales and the loans made on these homes are then used to build other homes. The program calls for the building of a series of homes, one at a time, in each of the communities of the county.

Once completed and sold, the money expended by the Housing Authority will be recaptured in a rotating fashion; then construction will begin on another house and will continue in the same manner throughout the county. About 18 per cent of the counties in the State have adopted this method of producing houses.

Appearing before the Sixty-fifth General Assembly at its opening session in January, 1947, Governor Green had only to refer to the record in the matter of his housing program for which he had had to fight so bitterly before its inauguration two years previously. He could, to use a well worn cliche, "point with pride." But, as he had known at the beginning, that victory of two years before was just an opening wedge. Tremendous things had been accomplished, but the problem of housing and of land clearance was by no means solved. In particular, the Governor was concerned with the slums of Chicago; with him slum clearance and adequate housing was not a political problem; he didn't care who got the credit just so long as something would be done — and doing things of the sort he had in mind takes money. Fortunately, Chicago had a Mayor, lately inducted into office, who was in no way politically minded, but was one hundred per cent civic-minded. Martin Kennelly saw eye-to-eye with Dwight Green on the need for private enterprise's co-operation in slum clearance and in the opening up of these readily accessible places to improvement in the form of modern housing plans. Kennelly agreed to do what his predecessor had declined to do — appoint a Land Clearance Commission and accept State aid for its operations.

The new housing and slum clearance bills presented to the Sixty-fifth Assembly — sponsored and prepared by the Governor — asked for a total of thirty millions. Of this sum fifteen millions were to be earmarked for land clearance, five millions for restoration housing (on what had been slum land), and ten millions for further grants along the line of the 1945 grants. In the matter of land clearance and restoration the communities accepting the State money had to match dollar for dollar.

Expenditure estimates were heavy; the bills were passed but the appropriations were cut one-third — to $20,000,-000. Of this $10,000,000 was set aside for land clearance,

$3,333,000 for restoration housing, and the balance for community distribution.

The Governor was not disheartened. You can do a lot with twenty millions though not as much as you can do with thirty millions. And once you start getting those slums out of the way and replacing eyesores with homes of cleanliness, comfort, and beauty, you have established a pattern by which the people, with the co-operation of their local and State governments, may hope to overcome the great problems of blighted areas, which confronts every major city in America.

== 32 ==

MILESTONES OF PROGRESS

A S A RESULT OF 20 YEARS RESIDENCE IN THE CITY
of Chicago, before he went to Springfield as
Governor, Dwight Green well understood that
the greatest need of his city, next to housing, was an
adequate transportation system. He had seen the tremendous expansion of the Midwestern metropolis, as it spread
across the prairies unhindered by any natural barriers of
hills or water, render obsolete the system of surface streetcars, elevated lines, and bus lines which had met fairly
adequately Chicago's transportation needs prior to World
War I.

He knew the financial and political history of Chicago
traction. He had seen the surface lines stymied by the
expiration of the 1907 ordinance twenty years later and the
inability of the company, the city government, and the
people to agree on a sound basis for their future developments. He had seen the elevated lines, once the pride of

Chicago, foiled by a depression which prevented their expansion to meet the spreading frontiers of the city at a time when the advent of the automobile had both established a new competition with public transit and had added hundreds of square miles to the territory which could be reached in the commuter's forty-five minutes from the heart of the city.

He had watched from the side lines during the sorry period when traction became a political football which was kicked about in every Chicago campaign. He had heard politicians rant about a five-cent fare, universal transfers, and higher wages for transit workers when simple arithmetic proved that not all — and probably none — of these goals could be achieved. In his campaign for Mayor of Chicago he had promised a sound solution of Chicago's local transportation, and he had meant to provide it.

He had not forgotten that promise when he went to Springfield as the State's chief executive. The problems of a war governor had prevented his attacking the traction dilemma in his first term but at the outset of his second administration, in 1945, he met it head on. The Illinois Commerce Commission had been forced to disapprove a unification plan proposed by the Chicago City Council because the capitalization which it proposed to fasten on the traction properties would have precluded a successful operation and modernization of the various lines. Meanwhile, the cars and tracks which were carrying the extra burden of increased numbers of war workers and the increased riding public resulting from the shortage of automobile tires and gasoline, was groaning under its added burden until it had almost reached the breaking point. There was no hope of new capital for either the streetcars or the elevated lines, which were in various types of receivership; five major attempts to work out a solution providing a unification with its intended economies and a financial foundation to permit the necessary expansion had failed. The situation was further complicated by the fact that any solution would require legislative action by a General Assembly dominated by downstate members who, not without reason, were suspicious of the honesty and the confidence of Chicago's local government. Party lines were only incidental to this fundamental sectional cleavage.

Nonetheless the Governor tackled the problem. Over the protest of sincere political advisers who told him he could not hope to retain the confidence of downstate Republicans in the General Assembly if he co-operated with Edward J. Kelly, then Mayor of Chicago and the head of the Democratic City Hall machine, he openly invited the Mayor to a conference on Chicago problems in the Executive Mansion. While cameras clicked and reporters wrote columns about this strange proceeding, the groundwork was laid for conferences which resulted in the enactment of legislation creating the Chicago Metropolitan Transit Authority. And despite predictions that it could not be done, this public municipal corporation — with power to acquire the local transit systems and to issue revenue bonds, payable out of operating income — in August 1947, took over the surface and elevated properties. Under the direction of its seven-man board, four appointed by the Mayor and three by the Governor, it began its great task of modernizing the service, eliminating needless competition, and providing the people of Chicago and its suburbs in Illinois with safe and fast transportation. There is still a tremendous job ahead of the new authority, but already new cars are operating on both the elevated and the surface lines, and a start has been made on a comprehensive program to replace many ancient trolley lines with modern bus transportation.

The onetime Wabash quarterback had kicked the traction football over the political fence, and seven businessmen of unquestioned integrity, wide experience, and exceptionally high ability, were working together without any thought of which political power — the Mayor or the Governor — had chosen them for the task.

While the Chicago traction program unfolded Governor Green was turning his attention to what might be termed the opposite extreme of the transportation system in Illinois. Illinois had been a pioneer in the construction of hard roads. Its network of major and secondary highways gave Illinois the same national leadership in the period of highway construction which it had earlier enjoyed in the days when most of the state's commerce was carried on water and later in the period of the great development of American railways. Yet the Governor who had carried brick for his grandfather, when the first pavement was laid in Ligonier, found when he got to Springfield that more than a hundred thousand Illinois farmers were cut off from the State's great highway system because the rural roads connecting the highways to their farms were undeveloped and often impassable for long periods of each year.

The Illinois Agricultural Association had been battling for more than a quarter of a century to correct this situation: their efforts had failed largely because such roads could not qualify for the funds from the Federal Government which were available to match State funds for highway construction raised from automobile licenses and the motor fuel tax. The Governor decided that the State had an obligation to make its highways accessible to all the people and that the State should meet this obligation even if no Federal help was available. He sponsored and obtained from the Sixty-fourth General Assembly, an appropriation of fifteen million dollars from the General Revenue funds of the State Treasury for a start on this program. Despite the handicaps of war and postwar shortages, hundreds of miles of all-weather farm-to-highway roads were constructed in 1946 and 1947, and a similar appropriation was passed by the Sixty-fifth General Assembly.

The year 1945 saw milestones of progress in still another field of transportation in Illinois. As recommended by the Governor in his second inaugural, the General Assembly authorized the creation of a separate Code Department of Aeronautics, and Illinois became the first state thus to recognize its responsibility to provide for the development of aviation facilities within its borders. The new department undertook the planning of a comprehensive program of State airports to meet the needs of the smaller as well as the larger communities of the state. State funds totaling three million dollars were allocated to the improvement of key airports in this system and have aided the construction and modernization of airports at various downstate cities, as well as at Chicago's lake-front island airport. In addition, in co-operation with Federal authorities, the State obtained for the University of Illinois a most modern airport at Champaign which both serves that community and provides a laboratory for the pioneer work of the University in aeronautical engineering and air commerce. The Illinois program has provided the impetus for the sound developments of both commercial and private flying, and the Governor's Beechcraft, in almost daily use in his journeys about the state, is an augur of the future of Illinois aviation.

Public health and public aid programs moved rapidly forward in Illinois even during the war. While Illinois has long enjoyed a favorable position in its public health achievements as measured by such standards as mortality rates and the number of cases of contagious disease, the war, with its shifting in population to new industrial centers, brought new problems. The cause of public health in the smaller communities was advanced by the adoption of legislation providing for the organization of county boards of health and permitting small counties to unite for this purpose. State diagnostic centers were established in sections with limited hospital facilities, particularly in southern Illinois. The public works budget adopted in 1947 provides for the construction of the first State hospitals for tubercular patients and also sets up a fund for State grants to match local and Federal funds in the construction of public and community hospitals.

In the field of public aid, the war and postwar administrations in Illinois have seen the establishment of a comprehensive program of aid to dependent children and increases in the State's contribution for old-age assistance and aid to the blind — not only to meet the increased cost of living, but also to provide additional funds for medical care for the recipients of State aid.

In a decade which has witnessed the greatest labor strife and unrest in the history of America, Illinois has been relatively free of strikes and disorders. The workers of Illinois have learned to have confidence in a Governor who backed up the assertion in his first inaugural that the prosperity of the State depended upon the prosperity of the workers, by the enactment of legislation establishing the prevailing wage for all workers in the State service or on work done by contract for the State, equal pay for equal work by women, and a series of enactments increasing the benefits and improving the administration of the State's workmen's compensation and unemployment insurance laws. At the state convention of the Illinois Federation of Labor in Peoria, on September 26, 1947, Dwight H. Green received the greatest ovation that body had ever paid a Governor in Illinois. Not for what he had done but for what he had prevented.

In his message at the opening session of the legislature in January, he had cautioned the Assembly against disturbing the sound labor peace which prevailed in Illinois. He had warned against yielding to the antilabor hysteria

tionment as well as state senatorial, although one session did pass a congressional reapportionment law which was thrown out by the Supreme Court on the grounds that it did not create properly contiguous and equal districts. Governor Green had seen three legislatures ignore his recommendations for reapportionment, and in the war sessions had accepted the situation in order to concentrate on immediate duties.

When he addressed the 1947 session, however, he had a new sense of the great need for action, especially on congressional reapportionment. In the campaign of 1946, he had assumed an obligation, as the now proven leader of the Republican party in his state, to elect as many Republican congressmen as possible. The Republican United States Senator C. Wayland Brooks had been returned to his seat in 1942. The Governor's effort necessarily was largely concentrated in Cook County, because all but one of the downstate districts already were represented by Republicans, while the only Republican Congressman from Cook County represented the North Shore suburban district, which also included Republican Lake County. In the course of that campaign, which resulted in Republican victory in five of the ten Cook County districts and the election of twenty Republicans in the Illinois delegation of twenty-six, the Governor learned two things. First, the failure to reapportion was being used effectively as a political weapon by the Democrats. Second, and more important, the gravest injustices resulting from that failure to reapportion were not between Chicago and downstate, but between districts entirely within Cook County.

The forty-six years which had elapsed since the last

redistricting had seen tremendous changes within Cook County. The Seventh district, which included the most rapidly growing wards on the Northwest Side of Chicago and the suburbs beyond them, now included a population of almost a million persons. The Sixth district, including old West Side areas from which there had been a steady exodus of population, now showed a population less than one-seventh of that size. Practically all districts were affected until approximately three-fourths of the people of Cook County lived in the five larger districts, one-fourth in the five smaller ones.

The Governor cited those discrepancies in his message to the General Assembly and pleaded for immediate action to correct them. At the same time he attempted to divorce congressional reapportionment from the more controversial issue of state redistricting, by proposing that the legislature should not consider that subject in this session but should create a Commission to consider the proposal of a new basis in electing the state legislature for later submission as an amendment to the State Constitution. The Governor's suggestions were received with polite attention and some applause by the downstate members of both parties, who no doubt made mental reservations that they would talk of that issue when the time came, using one or another of the means by which they had sidetracked or defeated reapportionment bills in the past.

They sat back and waited for the Governor's reapportionment bill to be introduced. It was not immediately forthcoming. The first intimation that the Governor was seriously pressing the plan came when it was learned that the chairmen of the Senate and House committees which would deal with such bills had been invited early in February to accompany the Governor on a trip to Washington where he was to deliver the Lincoln Day address arranged by the Republicans in Congress. In advance of that trip, the Governor had been in communication with the Republican Congressmen from Illinois. He knew that the opposition of individual Congressmen to the boundaries proposed for their own district had been an effective means of beating previous reapportionment plans. He therefore had asked the Congressmen to take the initiative in preparing a plan which would do substantial justice to all.

When the Governor and the legislators arrived in the national capital, they were presented with a redistricting map which the Congressmen themselves had prepared. It provided for 26 districts — 13 in Cook County, one of which included Lake County, and 13 downstate. Many of the Congressmen were by no means pleased with the way it might affect their personal political fortunes, but all had agreed that it was the right thing to do. The fairness with which it had been made was attested by the fact that the map drew practically no criticism from the Democratic members. This map became the basis of bills which were introduced in both the Senate and the House at Springfield.

For almost two months the bills slumbered in committee. Early in April, after the usual spring recess of the legislature for the municipal elections, the Governor undertook a personal campaign in behalf of the program. At weekly meetings with members of the Executive Committee of Republican Senators, he discussed various problems of the budget and the legislative program in which they were interested. Invariably he steered the discussion around to reapportionment. When he was met with statements from Senators that they could accept the principle of Congressional reapportionment, but they believed a better bill could be written, the Governor invited them to write one. When it became clear that efforts at amendment were accomplishing only delay, the Governor pleaded for action which would permit the bill to be voted up or down. He urged on the Republican members of the Senate the importance of passing the bill with at least the 26 votes required for its adoption coming from the Republican side of the body.

Eventually, on May 22, the Senate passed the bill very nearly in the form in which it had come from Washington. The vote was 35 to 9 with 26 Republicans voting in the affirmative.

Quite probably some of those votes were cast by reluctant downstaters who felt that this time it was the House's turn to administer the coup de grace to the reapportionment program. They relied upon their colleagues in the lower house to find means of choking the measure to death with amendments in the remaining few weeks of the session. Those hopes were dashed when it was revealed that the administration strategy was to abandon the dormant House bill and to move to advance the Senate bill to second reading in the House without reference to the committee.

Suddenly veteran downstate members who had successfully fought reapportionment for years realized that its passage was imminent. The Governor probably could muster enough loyal administration Republicans to obtain with Democratic help the 77 votes required for passage.

In their thoughts and actions on this subject, the foes of reapportionment were guided more by their emotions than by logic. Indeed with an almost religious fervor they huddled to prepare for battle. Late in May at a meeting of legislative leaders in the Executive Mansion to discuss the next day's program, one of the Governor's ablest and staunchest supporters suggested that perhaps he should not participate in the meeting since some of his fellow members were planning to do something against the Governor in which his conscience would force him to join. It was difficult to persuade him to accept the hospitality of the Mansion supper which concluded the conference.

On the morning of May 28 that "something" happened. When Representative Homer Harris, the majority leader, rose to make the routine request for unanimous consent that the House suspend the rules and proceed without reading the Journal of the previous day's session, several members were on their feet to object. It was the beginning of a filibuster, the favorite weapon of a legislative minority to prevent action by a majority. The objectors knew that actually the Journal of one day's session was never printed and on the members' desks until the afternoon of the following day. They knew, too, that the Journal of the preceding day contained the lengthy report of a special legislative committee which would consume many hours in reading by the clerks of the House.

Lacking unanimous consent the rules could be suspended only by the votes of a constitutional majority of the House — 77 votes. Enough Republicans had joined the revolt to prevent the suspension of the rules by Republican votes alone. The Democrats, constrained by political necessity to favor reapportionment, could not resist the political opportunity to permit the Republicans thus divided to hamstring themselves. Throughout the roll call, on the suspension of the rules, in which each of the filibusterers took their full five minutes allotted to each member to explain his vote, the Democrats sat silent, practically all of them failing to answer when their names were called. The motion to suspend the rules thus was lost, and with the Journal not there to be read, the House adjourned for the day.

The next day and the following legislative day, Monday, June 2, saw a repetition of the filibuster and the roll call. But this day the Journals of the two preceding days were at hand, and the Speaker ordered that they be read. Over a stormy undercurrent of parliamentary maneuvering, the reading clerks went on all that day and late into the afternoon of Tuesday when the filibusterers themselves finally waived the remainder of the performance in order that the House might adjourn for the annual softball game with the Senate.

The filibuster continued almost a week. Each roll call was an occasion for violent speeches explaining members' votes, and many of the downstaters bitterly denounced their Governor. "Dictator" was one of the milder terms they hurled at him. Representatives from Cook County became equally vehement. The Chicago press, denouncing the spectacle of the filibustering legislature, called upon the Governor to use all his political power against his opponents. The Governor remained calm; he continued his efforts to persuade the recalcitrants, but he refused to join in the name calling.

The MIDWESTERNER

On Wednesday, June 4, the House finally reached a roll call on the motion to advance the reapportionment bill to second reading. The motion carried. Subsequently, in committee-of-the-whole hearings, several series of amendments were introduced by various members, and all of them were voted down. On June 17, the House approved the Senate bill without change. The vote was 107 to 39, and 58 Republicans voted in the affirmative.

By this action the last hope of the opponents of reapportionment to defeat the measure was frustrated. Had the House amended the Senate bill in any way, it would have been necessary for the Senate to concur in the House amendments or for the House to recede from them if the Senate refused to concur; otherwise the bill would have had to go to conference. In any of these procedures the way would have been opened for new filibusters to kill the bill in the closing days of the session.

As it was, the bill now went to the Governor for his signature. His satisfaction in having achieved an Illinois goal which had seemed impossible for more than thirty years was rudely shaken when the bill was returned to him by the Attorney General, to whom it had been sent for technical approval before the Governor signed it. The Attorney General pointed out that the legislature had failed to include a portion of the township of Stickney in Cook County in any congressional district. The township of Stickney originally had been a rectangular area southwest of the city of Chicago. A large part of it had been detached from the township and annexed to the city of Chicago, becoming a part of the Thirteenth ward. The remainder of the township consisted of the village of

Stickney, in which most of its population resided, but certain areas remained outside the limits of that village. The bill, passed after such great effort, had placed the Thirteenth ward of Chicago in one district and the village of Stickney in another. Through an error in drafting — whose it has never been discovered — it had not placed the remainder of the township of Stickney in any district. The discovery of the error raised the serious question as to whether the new bill would be sustained by the Supreme Court.

On the afternoon of Tuesday, June 24, there was a most serious conference in the Executive Mansion. To have passed a corrected bill would have required action on three separate legislative days in each House. With the heavy calendar of the closing session, it was obviously impossible to do this. The result of the conference was the introduction in each House on the following day of resolutions which asserted it was the intention of the legislature to include the entire township of Stickney in the district where the village was mentioned. The Governor then signed the bill. In this unexpected emergency, his policy of remaining calm throughout the debate and filibuster on the reapportionment bill bore fruit. In large numbers the bitter foes of reapportionment joined with its champions in approving the corrective resolution. Also many of the opponents of the reapportionment program stood solidly for other bills in the Governor's legislative program in the final days of the session.

It remained for the Illinois Supreme Court to decide if the reapportionment bill was constitutional. In mid-November the court held that in spite of the trivial inaccuracies and the manner of their correction, the intention of the legislature was clear and the act was valid.

No court verdict was needed, however, to validate the fact that the patient and effective leadership of Dwight H. Green had finally broken down a barrier of sectional prejudice which had existed in Illinois for a generation. The way now has been opened for effective co-operation by all sections of the state to achieve by constitutional means agreement on real representative government for Illinois.

The *Chicago Daily News* hailed the act as "a belated victory for popular government" and pointed out that "Governor Green made congressional redistricting a major item on his 1947 legislative program" although "it was not popular with downstate Republicans. Illinois," the *News* continued, "has made a beginning toward restoring representative government."

Pointing out that the 1948 election of Illinois congressmen "will be a fair election — the first of its kind in nearly forty years," the *Chicago Tribune* added:

"It remained for Governor Green and a Republican General assembly to bring about the adoption of a redistricting measure that gave substantial equality of representation to all the people in Illinois. The achievement was the more commendable in that downstate, which lost representation, is overwhelmingly Republican in sentiment.

"For this great victory much credit must be given to all who had a part in it and above all to Governor Green, whose persistent efforts won passage of the redistricting act by the legislature."

*T*he November morning that the
Supreme Court announced its decision in the reapportionment case, Dwight Green was up to his neck in an event
typical of the extracurricular activities which had punctuated his administration as Governor. He was acting as host
and co-chairman at the National Aviation Clinic, a gathering of some six hundred top-flight executives and public
officials meeting to discuss every phase of national aviation
policy. It was probably the largest and most important convention ever held in Springfield, and, but for the precon-
vention organization supervised by the Governor, would
have far overtaxed the hotel and other facilities of the city.
Because no hotel dining room could accommodate the daily
luncheons or the annual banquet of the Clinic, the main floor
of the State Armory auditorium was converted into a dining-
room; a Chicago catering firm served the delegates and
their guests there, and the business sessions of the Clinic
were held in the chamber of the House of Representatives.
To their own amazement and to the surprise of the local
committees, the aviation magnates were able to report at
the close of the session that Green and Illinois had provided
them with the most comfortable and effective setting under
which the Clinic had ever been held.

At the same time, the Governor was directing preparations for a "Stars for Mercy" entertainment to be held in Chicago a month later, which was to jam the huge Chicago Stadium and net some $130,000 for the building fund sponsored by Chicago civic leaders for a new and greater Mercy Hospital in Chicago. That the Governor would undertake two outside activities of such magnitude at the close of a year which had marked the hardest legislative session of his career, and just before the opening of the campaign year in which he would have both to seek re-election and to lead the battle for his party's national ticket in Illinois, was typical of the energy and enthusiasm of the Midwesterner. He was never too busy to respond to an opportunity to assist in an important civic project or to do something for the cause of aviation, so dear to his heart.

Dwight Green by nature is not given to self-analysis, and he seldom has time to engage in it. To his associates, however, he typifies a living-and-working survival of the spirit of the midwestern pioneers — their friendliness and community loyalty, their unlimited faith in themselves and in the destiny of their country under its free system, and their willingness to do the spade work required for the success of any necessary undertaking.

He believes passionately that the preservation of that pioneer spirit is the hope of America and the world. In his talks to his close associates and in his public addresses, he frequently points out that today's difficulties seem insignificant compared with those overcome by the men and women who transformed America from a wilderness to a

[310]

land of freedom, culture, and prosperity. He lives by organization and teamwork. He is still essentially a quarterback — a quarterback who not only calls signals but also does his share of the blocking, tackling, and carrying of the ball. He loves fun but, although he has no greater appetite for work than his neighbors, he accepts the rigors of training and campaigning which he knows are essential to victory. And once he plunges into a job, its arduous details become a part of the team effort from which he gets his deepest thrills and satisfactions.

The narrative of the Midwesterner, who turned 51 on January 9, 1948, is not ended. Many acts of the drama remain to be written. But of this we may be certain — whatever action takes place in them will be largely determined by the principal actor.